MW00475989

spooky trails and tall tales
CALIFORNIA

Help Us Keep This Guide Up to Date

Every effort has been made by the author and editors to make this guide as accurate and useful as possible. However, many things can change after a guide is published.

We would appreciate hearing from you concerning your experiences with this guide and how you feel it could be improved and kept up to date. While we may not be able to respond to all comments and suggestions, we'll take them to heart, and we'll also make certain to share them with the author. Please send your comments and suggestions to the following address:

FalconGuides
Reader Response/Editorial Department
246 Goose Lane
Guilford, CT 06437

Thanks for your input!

spooky trails and tall tales

CALIFORNIA

Hiking the Golden State's Legends, Hauntings, and History

TOM OGDEN

FALCON

GUILFORD, CONNECTICUT

For Randy Landenheim-Gil

An imprint of The Rowman & Littlefield Publishing Group, Inc.
4501 Forbes Blvd., Ste. 200
Lanham, MD 20706
www.rowman.com
Falcon and FalconGuides are registered trademarks and Make Adventure Your Story is a trademark
of The Rowman & Littlefield Publishing Group, Inc.

Distributed by NATIONAL BOOK NETWORK

Copyright © 2020 Tom Ogden

Maps by The Rowman & Littlefield Publishing Group, Inc.

All rights reserved. No part of this book may be reproduced in any form or by any electronic or
mechanical means, including information storage and retrieval systems, without written permission
from the publisher, except by a reviewer who may quote passages in a review.

British Library Cataloguing in Publication Information available

Library of Congress Control Number: 2020942014

ISBN 978-1-4930-4245-6 (paper)
ISBN 978-1-4930-4246-3 (electronic)

The author and The Rowman & Littlefield Publishing Group, Inc. assume no liability for accidents
happening to, or injuries sustained by, readers who engage in the activities described in this book.

Contents

CONTENTS

1. Pacific Northwest

2. The Cascades, the Sierra Nevada, and Death Valley

3. Bay Area

4. Greater Los Angeles

5. Inland Empire

6. Greater San Diego

Acknowledgments

To my friends Mark Willoughby, Joan Lawton, and Michael Kurland, thank you for taking my panicked calls when I wanted to run a passage by you or was struggling to find just the right word. Thank you, too, for pushing me this past year during my endless procrastination.

Thanks to everyone who forwarded me news stories about spooky happenings, shared their personal ghost stories, or described trails I was unable to visit. And, of course, thanks to all of you who graciously supplied me with your trail photos to illustrate the book.

Finally, thanks go out to my editor, David LëGere; former editors Evan Helmlinger (who brought me the project) and Ursula Cary; production editors Kristen Mellitt and Meredith Dias; copy editor Brooke Goode; layout artist Joanna Beyer; and cartographer Melissa Baker.

PHOTO COURTESY OF CHRISTINE COX

Introduction

I T'S SAID THAT ghosts are everywhere, and hiking trails are no exception. *Spooky Trails and Tall Tales* is for avid hikers, armchair backpackers, and paranormal investigators alike. In the coming pages, we'll be exploring more than a hundred haunted trails scattered throughout half of California's fifty-eight counties.

The presence of ghosts on these paths shouldn't be surprising. California's original inhabitants, the Native Americans, believed in the existence of both ancestral and divine spirits. It's little wonder that stories of apparitions permeate their culture and "populate" the land on which they lived. Many of today's ghosts date to the arrival of Europeans, especially the periods of Spanish exploration, pioneer settlement, the gold rush, and the Old West, and new phantoms are being added to California pathways every day.

Whether you believe the ghost stories is up to you. But if you bump into something otherworldly on a trail, don't say you weren't warned.

Spooky Trails and Tall Tales is divided into six parts, and each one is dedicated to a specific region of California. Numerous haunted places have been reported within a few miles of California's three major population centers—San Francisco, Los Angeles, and San Diego—but plenty of earthbound spirits can be found in the less densely inhabited parts of the state as well: the Pacific Northwest, the mountains, and the deserts.

The types of paths in *Spooky Trails and Tall Tales* differ as much as the spectres that haunt them. You'll find the routes vary in length, difficulty, amount of foot traffic, accessibility, necessary mountaineering skills, and environments in which you'll be hiking. Although this book is primarily about walking trails, you'll also find a few related ghost stories about phantom-filled roads, intersections, bridges, waterfalls, and beaches.

Note that the GPS positions cited in this book should be considered accurate but approximate. The GPS is a modern miracle, but even with all its advantages it's sometimes difficult to pinpoint an exact location, especially something as precise as a trailhead, a waterfall, or a scenic overlook. Two hikers standing just a few yards apart have been known to get wildly different readings. The main sources for the coordinates I cite are AllTrails .com and Google Maps.

Please be aware that many of the trails and parks mentioned in this book have restricted hours, often prohibiting visitors from dusk to dawn. There are no hikes in *Spooky Trails* that are on private property or require you to break the law. I've noted the few places that the "No Trespassing" or "Do Not Enter" signs are invalid and can be ignored.

Also, some sites require a National Forest Adventure Pass to park on the property, and the pass should be clearly displayed inside your vehicle. There are both one-day and annual passes available. Check the USDA Forest Service website (fs.usda.gov) to find out which California recreational areas require the pass as well as where to purchase them. Among other places, you can pick one up at an REI if there's one near you, whether you're a member of the co-op or not.

Other permits or fees may apply for certain recreational areas, including the national parks. It's always best to check before leaving home.

The hauntings in *Spooky Trails and Tall Tales* run the gamut from eerie sounds and disembodied voices to visible apparitions. And then there are the "tall tales" about cryptids—strange creatures not recognized by scientists and whose existence is based on legends, eyewitness reports, or indirect, inconclusive evidence. These are the stories of mythic beings such as giant serpents, hunchbacked beasts, and Bigfoot.

Finally, these stories are told for entertainment purposes. It's assumed that anyone who takes these hikes is experienced and well prepared before setting out and that the hiker takes responsibility for any accidents or loss that may occur.

In other words, be safe out there. Wherever your adventures take you, have fun!

Preface

D0 YOU BELIEVE in ghosts? If you do, you're not alone. According to recent polls, 45 percent of those surveyed think that ghosts exist. Almost 20 percent say they've encountered one.

Ghost enthusiasts already accept that spirits are real, and many also think there's at least a possibility that other strange beings such as witches, vampires, and Bigfoot are out there as well. Devotees already know that phantoms and mythic creatures haunt trails and parks every bit as much as they do houses, cemeteries, and hotels, and many hikers, backpackers, and campers—if pressed—will admit they, too, sometimes see or hear weird, unexplainable stuff "go bump in the night."

What believers and skeptics alike want is proof or at least some sort of explanation for the phenomena. What are ghosts? And why do they return?

First of all, let's eliminate what ghosts are *not*. They're not deliberate hoaxes or deceptions, such as the Amityville Horror, retouched photos, intentional double exposures, or images that have been digitally altered.

Sometimes what seems otherworldly is just an optical illusion, such as a boat over the horizon that appears to be a wispy, phantom ship due to refraction in the atmosphere. (Think Flying Dutchman.) Similarly, what people see could be a hallucination, such as the mind creating a nonexistent oasis out of heat waves rising from a scorching desert.

Sadly, some folks are mentally unbalanced and can't tell the difference between fantasy and reality. Being sick or making even a minor change in diet can also affect a person's perceptions. Charles Dickens understood that when writing *A Christmas Carol* back in 1843. The author has Scrooge dismiss Marley's ghost as mere indigestion by saying, "You may be an undigested bit of beef, a blot of mustard, a crumb of cheese, a fragment of underdone potato. There's more of gravy than of grave about you, whatever you are!"

So what *is* a ghost? The most common definition is that of the spirit, essence, aura, or soul of a deceased person. Detailing their differences in meaning is far beyond the scope of this book, as is the discussion of whether ghosts have returned from the Other Side or are earthbound and never departed. Then, some apparitions are active and interact with the living, but residual spirits repeat the same actions over and over as if they're on a film loop. It's also unknown why some people can see spectres and others only hear their disembodied voices, feel uneasy, or simply have a sense that "something's not right." And that's just touching the surface of ghost theory.

Just as interesting as the nature of apparitions are the reasons they would want to return to the world of the living. Believe it or not, there are paranormal clubs whose members discuss this and similar issues. (The first such association, the Society for Psychical Research, was established in London in 1882 in response to the claims coming out of séances being conducted in Victorian England.) After hearing hundreds of first-person accounts, researchers began to delineate why spirits return:

- It's the anniversary of an important event.
- To impart a message or give a warning.
- To comfort those left behind.
- To right a wrong, solve a mystery, or exact revenge.
- The spirit suffered a major physical trauma at the site, such as death, imprisonment, or burial.
- The spirit experienced a burst of great emotion there, such as ecstasy or heartbreak.
- The spirit frequented the place and felt at home, safe, happy, or loved.

- The spirit is unable to "cross over" without guidance.
- The spirit died so suddenly it doesn't know it's dead.
- The spirit just wants to be remembered.

Every ghost story in the coming chapters fits into one or more of these categories.

Now if we can only figure out how to explain Bigfoot.

Pacific Northwest

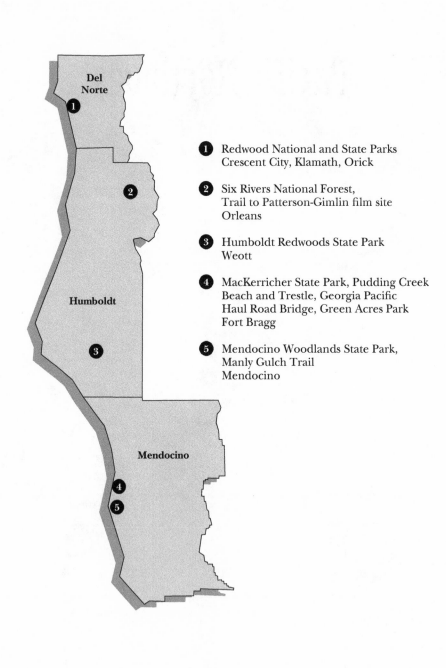

1 Redwood National and State Parks
Crescent City, Klamath, Orick

2 Six Rivers National Forest,
Trail to Patterson-Gimlin film site
Orleans

3 Humboldt Redwoods State Park
Weott

4 MacKerricher State Park, Pudding Creek
Beach and Trestle, Georgia Pacific
Haul Road Bridge, Green Acres Park
Fort Bragg

5 Mendocino Woodlands State Park,
Manly Gulch Trail
Mendocino

Indigenous Spirits

Redwood National and State Parks
Crescent City, Klamath, Orick, Del Norte County

Humboldt Redwoods State Park
Weott, Humboldt County

ICTURE A GIANT redwood. A single tree, 350 feet tall and 20 feet in diameter. Now picture thousands upon thousands of them. Prior to 1850, these magnificent redwoods, the tallest trees on earth, covered 20 million acres of the Northern California coast. Today, less than 10 percent of these old-growth mammoths still exist.

The redwood is a species of sequoia but is taller and more slender than its counterpart, the giant sequoia. Redwoods are always found below 3,000 feet and need a warm, moist climate to survive. In California they can only grow on a narrow strip about 500 miles long bordering the Pacific Ocean, from Monterey to just past the Oregon border. (The giant sequoia is found in drier climates farther inland and at higher elevations.)

The indigenous inhabitants of the coast were the Chilula, Karuk, Tolowa, Wiyot, and Yurok peoples. Of these, the Yurok was the largest tribe, with about 2,500 members. It's estimated that the ancestors of all these tribes had arrived in the area about 3,000 years before the arrival of Europeans.

As recently as two centuries ago, the redwood's place in the ecosystem seemed secure. Then came the California gold rush at Sutter's Mill in 1848 and a second one, minor and short-lived, that started two years later along the Trinity River. The rush was over by 1855, so many former prospectors stayed on to become lumberjacks. The redwood became a natural target. The trees were admired not for their beauty but for the amount of wood they could supply. Plus, the redwoods were plentiful, and they could be sawn into planks of unprecedented length.

Uncontrolled clear-cut logging began to decimate the forests, and by the turn of the twentieth century, it was apparent that something had to be done if the grand species were to be preserved. In 1918 the Save the Redwoods League was formed and, due in large part to its efforts, California created the Prairie Creek, Del Norte Coast, and Jedediah Smith Redwoods State Parks to protect the coastal sequoia. In 1968 the federal government combined the parks and added additional land to establish Redwood National and State Parks. The United Nations named the collected parks a World Heritage Site in 1980.

There are more than 200 established trails in Redwood National and State Parks, so when rangers are asked which ones to take, they suggest you make your selections based on such factors as your available time and fitness level, whether there any specific trees or groves you wish to see, and whether you have special needs. Dogs are not allowed on any of the trails in the Redwood National and State Parks.

If the trails and trees in Redwood National Park aren't enough for you, travel about 90 miles south on US 101 until you reach Humboldt Redwoods State Park. It has more than 100 miles of marked trails and is situated between the towns of Pepperwood to the north and Phillipsville to the south. The park headquarters are located between Weott and Myers Flat along a remarkable 32-mile stretch of scenic road known as the Avenue of the Giants.

The so-called "avenue," technically CA 254, was a wagon and stage-coach route in the 1880s, and it more or less parallels US 101. Whether you're going to Humboldt Redwoods State Park to hike, cycle, ride horse-back, or simply marvel at the redwood trees, a slow drive along the full length of the Avenue of the Giants is highly recommended.

Of course, loggers had their eyes on these redwoods as well. Here, too, the Save the Redwoods League came to the rescue. The organization acquired its first grove in the Weott area in 1921. Six years later they managed to buy Pacific Lumber's vast acreage. In the ensuing decades, various parties were able to add more property, and today Humboldt State Park has about 53,000 acres. Seventeen thousand of them contain old-growth redwood. Rockefeller Forest alone covers 10,000 of those acres, making it the largest concentrated old-growth redwood forest in the world.

No matter where you encounter the redwoods, it's impossible to view them without feeling a sense of awe and even reverence. As your eyes strain to follow the monumental trunks upward, it's easy to imagine the trees reaching all the way to the heavens.

The Yurok, along with other Native American tribes, considered all of the redwoods to be sacred, and they believed the trees contained living spirits. It was thought that the entity remained in the wood even after the tree was felled. As a result, redwoods were only cut for the most important purposes, such as building shelter. Those who used the wood to carve canoes always left a small wooden knob in the bottom of the dugout so that the tree's spirit had a place to reside. It was feared that without the protective spirit aboard, an evil force could seize the canoe and its occupants.

Many modern visitors to the redwood groves have claimed they've seen eerie, silent human figures drifting through the forests, far off the marked trails. Some think they're apparitions of long-dead Native Americans returning to their homes. Others think the phantoms are sinister because they're often seen wearing hooded robes or shrouds that hide their features, and no one has managed to get a close look at any of their faces. Also, quite a few people have reported having migraines or frightening visions after encountering the eerie creatures.

Perhaps the identity of the redwood revenants will always remain a mystery. As poet Robert Frost observed, "The woods are lovely, dark and deep."

Haunted Trails

Redwood National and State Parks
Redwood National and State Parks span three regions geographically, each with a small town that acts as a base for visitors: Crescent City (home to the park service headquarters) to the north, Klamath in the central section, and Orick to the south.

Located in Jedediah Smith Redwoods State Park, Boy Scout Trail is a 2.8-mile out-and-back path with a parking lot and a marked trailhead on Howland Hill Road. It's a moderate-difficulty track with some switchbacks and steep grades, though there's only a slight change in elevation. About 2.5 miles down the path there's an unmarked spur trail leading to Boy Scout Tree, so named because it was discovered by a scoutmaster. The tree is a rare double redwood: two towering trees that share a common trunk and root system. **Trailhead GPS: N41 46.132' / W124 06.635'**

Cathedral Trees Trail is located in Prairie Creek Redwoods State Park. It's a moderate, 3-mile out-and-back walk noted for its "cathedral groves," or clusters of trees. The marked trailhead begins at the Big Tree Wayside parking area, but the trail can also be accessed from Elk Prairie Trail or the Prairie Creek Visitor Center. **Trailhead GPS: N41 21.800' / W124 01.365'**

Damnation Creek Trail can be found in Del Norte Coast Redwoods State Park. Although it's only 2.2 miles long, the out-and-back trail is strenuous, dropping a thousand feet as hikers maneuver several switchbacks and steep grades from the forest to a tide pool on the Pacific shore. Check maritime tables to arrive at the beach during low tide. The trailhead is at milepost 16.0 on US 101. **Trailhead GPS: N41 38.873' / W124 06.785'**

Located in Del Norte Coast Redwoods State Park, Hobbs Wall Trail is an uneven, 3.4-mile looped path of moderate difficulty with lots of well-maintained bridges. One of the park's oldest trails, it's named for the two major lumber companies in Del Norte in the 1860s. As the track descends, you pass from old- to new-growth redwood. The trailhead is located off Mill Creek Campground. **Trailhead GPS: N41 42.003' / W124 07.158'**

Lady Bird Johnson Grove Trail is an easy 1.3-mile heavily trafficked loop trail located off Bald Hills Road in Redwood National Park. **Trailhead GPS: N41 18.232' / W124 01.107'**

Leiffer and Ellsworth Loop Trail is in Jedediah Smith Redwoods State Park. This 2.2-mile loop trail has some grades, but they're not too steep. The path starts on a section of the Crescent City Park Road built in the 1800s. It descends into a canyon under a canopy of old-growth redwood. The trailhead is off Walker Road. **Trailhead GPS: N41 49.003' / W124 06.734'**

Located in Jedediah Smith Redwoods State Park, Simpson-Reed Trail is an easy, level, 1-mile loop trail. It boasts a thick grove of redwoods interspersed with hemlock trees, brush, and ferns. It also has a stream winding among several fallen redwoods. The trailhead is accessed from Walker Road off US 199. **Trailhead GPS: N41 48.745' / W124 06.532'**

Stout Memorial Grove Trail is also situated in Jedediah Smith Redwoods State Park. Clara Stout gave this 44-acre grove to the Save the Redwoods League in 1929 in memory of her late husband, lumber baron Frank D. Stout. Many consider this to be the core of the Jedediah Smith Redwoods preserve. An easy 0.7-mile loop begins at a parking lot off Howland Hill Road. **Trailhead GPS: N41 47.362' / W124 05.064'**

Trillium Falls Trail is in Redwood National Park. Although considered to be of moderate difficulty, this 2.6-mile loop path has a few steep grades. The trail features several species of trees in addition to old-growth redwoods. There's also a 10-foot waterfall. **Trailhead GPS: N41 47.362' / W124 05.064'**

West Ridge Trail is a 5-mile, moderately trafficked loop trail in Prairie Creek Redwoods State Park. It's rated to be of moderate difficulty with a few steep grades (including an initial ascent) and switchbacks. It doesn't get much better than this trail if you want to see old-growth redwoods in relative solitude. It's possible to link West Ridge Trail with the James Irvine and Friendship Ridge Trails to create a 12.5-mile loop. And for backpackers, both the Ossagon and Miners Ridge Trails branch off West Ridge Trail and lead to campgrounds. **West Ridge Trailhead GPS: N41 21.848' / W124 01.372'**

For more information about Redwood National and State Parks, check the park's website at nps.gov/redw/index.htm. You'll find a list of ranger-recommended trails at nps.gov/redw/planyourvisit/hiking.htm.

Humboldt Redwoods State Park

Founders Grove Nature Trail is a 0.5-mile loop trail that starts on Dyerville Loop Road, just north of Mahan's Plaque Trail. The 362-foot Dyerville Giant, now fallen, can be seen along this path. The short loop is an easy walk and is heavily trafficked, in part because parking and restroom facilities are available close to the trailhead. **Trailhead GPS: N40 21.161' / W123 55.427'**

Mahan Plaque Trail is a 1-mile loop trail of moderate difficulty with a trailhead on the Avenue of the Giants. There is a pullout along the shoulder of the road about 5.5 miles north of Weott. There are no restrooms. **Trailhead GPS: N40 20.373' / W123 55.665'**

A short path runs between these two trails. If you're starting from Founders Grove, the connecter trail will be about halfway around the loop. If you start from the Mahan Plaque trailhead, the path will fork about

about 0.1 mile into your hike. Mahan Plaque Trail turns sharply to your right. To reach Founders Grove Trail, continue going straight and then veer left.

Brochures pointing out notable landmarks are available at the park's visitor center in Weott and at both ends of the Avenue of the Giants. **Southern entrance GPS: N40 11.066' / W123 46.775'; northern entrance GPS: N40 26.638' / W124 01.855'**

Don't worry if you miss these turnoffs. There are plenty of access routes to CA 254 from US 101. More information about Humboldt Redwoods State Park can be obtained online at parks.ca.gov/?page_id=425.

Bigfoot

Six Rivers National Forest, Trail to Patterson-Gimlin film site
Orleans, Humboldt County

LMOST EVERY CIVILIZATION throughout history has had legends about strange creatures that walked the earth. In Greek and Roman mythology, there was the Griffin, the Minotaur, Pegasus, and centaurs. European fairy tales are full of giants, ogres, mermaids, and trolls, just to name a few.

One unusual being that still appears in the folklore of modern cultures is an apelike, humanoid animal that populates dense, secluded forests and remote mountainsides. These cryptids are incapable of speech, although they've been known to let out bloodcurdling howls. There have been very few reports of their being violent, however, and they are amazingly elusive.

These hairy beasts have been called by different names. In early European folklore, they were known only as "wild men" or "hairy men," similar in description to the woodland satyrs or fauns of antiquity. Tibet has its Yeti, or Abominable Snowman. And North America has its Sasquatch. In fact, "sasquatch" means "wild man" in the language of the Salish, who were Native Americans living in the area of what is now Vancouver. In the Florida Everglades, the Sasquatch is known as a Skunk Ape. And throughout California, the Pacific Northwest, and, indeed, most of the United States, it's known as Bigfoot.

Native American stories of the North American Sasquatch long preceded the coming of Western trappers, pioneers, and missionaries. Although the creatures were vicious in some legends and benign or even shy in others, their physical appearance was almost identical from tribe to tribe. The creature was usually described as being about 7 feet tall and covered in black, brown, or slightly reddish hair. It was bipedal and walked upright.

Of course, there have always been doubters that such a being exists. But the modern tales of Bigfoot date to August 27, 1958, when Jerry Crew, a bulldozer operator in a lumber camp located in Six Rivers National Forest, noticed several footprints in the ground that were much too large to have been made by a human.

Six Rivers National Forest was established by President Truman in 1947, fashioned from portions of three other national forests—Klamath, Siskiyou, and Trinity. It's so named because six waterways pass through the forest or along its borders. And it's huge: Less than 50 miles inland from the Redwood National and State Parks, Six Rivers National Forest is ten times the size of its neighbor. The woodland contains more than a million acres, 137,000 of which are old-growth forest. Spread over four counties, Six Rivers has plenty of spots for hiking, camping, fishing, and simply enjoying the scenic splendor. The national forest's main headquarters is in Eureka.

But back to Jerry Crew. He immediately showed the massive footprints to his supervisor, and soon his coworkers were sharing stories about similar prints they had seen in other logging sites. Before long, the men were referring to the enormous but never-seen creature that made them as Big Foot. (At some point, the press merged the words into the more economical name Bigfoot.)

A month after his first discovery, Crew spotted a similar set of tracks running alongside Bluff Creek Road, just off CA 96. He traced an outline of one of the prints and took it to Bob Titmus, an area taxidermist. Unable to make a judgment from the crude sketch alone, Titmus taught Crew how to make a plaster cast of the impression.

The resulting model was between 16 and 18 inches long (sources vary) and 7 inches wide. Crew showed it to Titmus and another taxidermist, Al Corbett, but they were unimpressed. They concluded that Crew was the victim of a practical joke. Nevertheless, Titmus promised to visit the worksite to see the actual prints for himself. Eventually he did, and it changed his mind: He decided the prints were not a prank.

Andrew Ganzoli, a columnist for the *Humboldt Times* (precursor to today's Eureka *Times-Standard*) decided to drop in on the logging camp himself after receiving several tips about the Bigfoot brouhaha from Betty Allen, a Willow Creek resident and correspondent to the newspaper. Ganzoli felt that, if nothing else, it would make a fun human interest story. His article, along with a photo of Crew holding his cast of the footprint, appeared on the front page of the *Times* in early October 1958. Almost immediately, the story was picked up by wire services and was printed in newspapers across the country.

Interest soon waned, but Bigfoot fever swept the nation again, nine years later, when Roger Patterson and Robert "Bob" Gimlin announced they had captured a female Bigfoot on film. The encounter had allegedly occurred along Bluff Creek between one and two o'clock on the afternoon of October 20, 1967. Shot on grainy Kodachrome II color film, the movie is now referred to as the Patterson-Gimlin film (or PGF). A mere 59.5 seconds of footage—just 954 frames—show the gorilla-like animal walking away from Patterson, who was the cameraman. During that minute, the Sasquatch turns to the camera three times. The two men attempted to follow "Patty," as they nicknamed the creature, by following its tracks, but they lost its trail. Patterson also recorded the footprints on film and made casts of two of them.

There are skeptics as to what the film allegedly shows, of course. Stan Winston, an Oscar-winning special-effects man and makeup artist, declared that the Sasquatch in the film is "a guy in a bad hair suit," and in 1998 a man named Bob Heironimus told the press that he was the person inside the outfit. In 2002 Philip Morris, a prominent costumer in North Carolina, revealed that he provided the suit to Patterson. Whether real or a hoax, the Patterson-Gimlin film is still touted as the first footage ever shot of Bigfoot.

Since the PGF surfaced, other folks have produced video and film they say captures the evasive creature as well. A quick search on YouTube will provide several examples. Podcasts and conventions of believers have made Bigfoot a niche industry. But no town is more associated with the Sasquatch than Willow Creek, California.

The small mountain community of about 1,700 residents lies within Six Rivers National Forest and contains one of its four regional ranger stations. Located at the intersection of CA 96 and CA 299, Willow Creek has fully embraced its reputation as the Bigfoot Capital of the World. It's home to a Bigfoot museum and holds an annual "Bigfoot Daze" festival in September.

So if it's Bigfoot you're after, Willow Creek makes a perfect jumping-off point for your search. From Willow Creek, drive north on CA 96 through the Hoopa Valley Reservation. As with other tribes in the Pacific Northwest, the Sasquatch has been part of the Hoopa, or Hupa, mythology since time immemorial.

Just past the Hoopa village of Weitchpec, you'll enter Six Rivers National Forest. You're now in Big Foot Country. It's 12 miles from Weitchpec to Orleans, which is the closest village to where the Patterson-Gimlin film was shot. There are also a number of nearby campgrounds, including Aikens Creek, E-Ne-Nuck, and Fish Lake Campgrounds. The northern terminus of the Bigfoot Scenic Highway (as this 89-mile stretch of CA 96 is known) is Happy Camp, where you can pose next to a 20-foot sculpture of the beast.

Is Bigfoot real? Well, when asked that question in a 2002 interview on National Public Radio, primate expert Jane Goodall said, "I'm sure they exist." She followed that with a small laugh, however, and added, "Well, I'm a romantic, so I always wanted them to exist."

Haunted Trails

All of the trails in Six Rivers National Forest (especially along CA 96) are in Big Foot Country, but the hike that will probably be of the most interest to Sasquatch seekers is the one to the Patterson-Gimlin film site.

Unfortunately, the trail isn't marked, and access to it is from a berm at the dead end of a series of difficult, interconnected forest roads north of CA 96. The berm, a large dirt embankment at the end of FR 12N13H, was bulldozed into place to stop vehicular traffic from going any farther, but there is enough parking space for about six cars. **Trailhead GPS: N41 26.501' / W123 41.966'**

The Bluff Creek Project has dedicated itself to verifying and mapping the location where the Patterson-Gimlin film was shot. The organization shares its findings at http://bluffcreekproject.blogspot.com/p/blog-page_22.html. The following directions, including the GPS coordinates, are paraphrased from their instructions.

On the other side of the berm, you'll find a trail that was originally a logging road down to Bluff Creek. It's a 30- to 45-minute walk to where the PGF was shot. At one point along the way, there's a ravine where the old road has washed out. It's best to use the path on the left side of the gulley as you continue down toward Bluff Creek. Once you reach the water, walk upstream until you get to a small set of rapids and a little pool. (There's often an exposed gravel bar next to the stream.) From the pool, just ahead to your left, you should be able to see a trail leading up to the flat cliff where Bigfoot appeared. There's usually a bottle or two hanging from the trees, left behind by others, to mark the location. Patterson was at creek level when he shot his famous footage. **Filming GPS: N41 26.412' / W123 42.115'**

The Bigfoot Museum in Willow Creek might be helpful with directions to this and other promising trails in the area. Make sure to check on weather and road conditions before setting out. Some of the roads are gated from late September to early June due to snow.

The Patterson-Gimlin film can be viewed several places online. The complete footage can be seen, for example, at https://www.youtube.com/watch?v=YQqt3QqHhM8. Bigfoot appears at about the 2:34 mark. A stabilized and enhanced version of just the Sasquatch portion can be found at https://www.youtube.com/watch?v=Q60mSMmhTZU.

3

The Phantoms of Fort Bragg

MacKerricher State Park, Pudding Creek Beach and Trestle,
Georgia Pacific Haul Road Bridge, Green Acres Park
Fort Bragg, Mendocino County

WHEN MOST PEOPLE hear "Fort Bragg," they think about the army base in North Carolina. It's one of the largest military installations in the world, with more than 50,000 service members stationed there on active duty.

The *haunted* Fort Bragg, however, is a city on the California coast, situated in Mendocino County on CA 1. The town grew out of a US garrison that once stood on the site, and it was named for the same person as the North Carolina fort: Captain Braxton Bragg, a distinguished veteran of the Mexican-American War. (The fort in North Carolina grew out of Camp Bragg, an artillery training ground established in 1918, more than fifty years after Bragg became a general in the Confederate Army. There has been discussion in recent years of removing the names of Confederate officers from US military installations, including Fort Bragg.)

Before the arrival of pioneers, the region was home to Pomo and Yuki Native Americans. In 1856, not long after the start of the California Indian Wars, the US Bureau of Indian Affairs relocated the native inhabitants to Mendocino Indian Reservation, which was established at the mouth of the Noyo River. A military outpost, Fort Bragg, was constructed where Pudding Creek emptied into the sea.

Of course, all of that is ancient history. The garrison was shuttered by 1867. Two years after that, the reservation itself was closed and its land offered up for sale. Lumber became the big local industry, followed by commercial fishing. Today, the city of Fort Bragg is a popular tourist destination, with one of its most notable attractions being MacKerricher State Park.

The coastal recreational area begins about 3.5 miles north of Fort Bragg and stretches 9 miles up to Ten Mile River. The property had been part of a ranch owned by Duncan and Jessie MacKerricher, who had moved from Canada in 1864. Their heirs sold the land to the state in 1949.

The southern end of the park is noted for its rocky cliffs and many small beaches, and it's along one of those bluffs that people see Fort Bragg's most famous ghosts. Legend has it that Lt. Col. George Custer and his 7th Cavalry Regiment traveled through the region during the Indian Wars and at one point had to make their way up the bluffs overlooking Pudding Creek. It's said that people standing on Pudding Creek Beach occasionally see the spectres of Custer and his men scrambling up the face of the steep ridge in an eternal replay of the event.

The spectres are also spotted by folks crossing the old wooden Pudding Creek Trestle, which was built in 1915. It was originally part of the Ten Mile Railroad, used to haul timber into town—as its name suggests—from 10 miles north. The 527-foot-long span is 44 feet high, supported by 34 upright poles. There's no possibility of the sudden appearance of a train, however: The bridge was put out of service in 1949. A new planked walkway has been laid across the top of the trestle from end to end.

Will you actually see the ghosts of any military men or horses from either of these locations? Who knows? The whole tale about Custer may be apocryphal. He wasn't sent to fight in the Indian Wars until 1866, and he famously died in the Montana Territory on June 25, 1876, at the Battle of the Little Bighorn (commonly known as Custer's Last Stand). His ten years in the West were spent primarily in Kansas, Colorado, Indian Territory (part of present-day Oklahoma), the Dakota Territory, and, finally, the Montana Territory. There is little evidence to support the claim that he served in the California Indian Wars or, indeed, ever visited the Fort Bragg area. But let's not let facts get in the way of a good story.

There's another haunted bridge in Fort Bragg: the Georgia Pacific Haul Road Bridge. According to local folklore, sometime in the past a man was attacked on the bridge, dragged off, tortured, and then killed. And as if that weren't enough, the murderer(s) then hanged his corpse from a tree. It's said the victim wasn't very pleasant when he was alive, but his apparition certainly isn't. The spirit, smelling of decomposing flesh, has shoved or scratched people walking across the bridge. Even dogs don't like to use it.

There are lots of other unidentified spooks in and around Fort Bragg. Almost all of them are dressed in gold rush or Victorian-era garb. One of the most frequently seen ghosts is that of a young woman in mid-nineteenth-century clothing. She wanders aimlessly through the state park, approaches strangers, and asks them whether they've seen her boy-friend. According to an old wives' tale, she's unaware that her beau was killed in the Civil War.

Finally, you'll have to stay someplace after a busy day of ghost hunting, right? There are many camping options close to Fort Bragg, including the Pinewood and Surfwood Campgrounds, both of which are located within MacKerricher State Park. But also consider Green Acres Campground and RV Park. There have been reports of a spirit roaming its grounds.

The Green Acres ghost is never seen, and its gender is disputed, but people hear the spectre's disembodied humming—always the same unrecognizable tune, repeated over and over. The phenomenon reportedly occurs at different times of the night, and a sudden chill often accompanies the sound.

Among paranormalists, it's believed that such an isolated "cold spot" signals the presence of a spirit or could even be its icy touch. Others think these spots serve as portals between the worlds of the living and the dead. Then again, sometimes a chill is just a chill.

Haunted Trails

One the best places to stand while looking for the ghosts of Custer and his soldiers is Pudding Creek Beach. It's located at the end of a sandy cove where the stream meets the Pacific. Depending upon the season, though, there may not be much of a creek, or the water may pool up on the beach and never reach the ocean. There are several unmarked walking trails from the beach to the top of the bluff. One of these paths *could* be the spot where Custer and the regiment climbed the cliffs. We can't be sure because there's no reliable record as to where—or if—the ascent took place. **Pudding Creek Beach GPS: N39 27.540' / W123 48.519'**

You can begin your walk across Pudding Creek Trestle from either side. It may be more convenient to start from the southern end, where there's a small public parking lot for about twenty vehicles. It's located at 1000 MacKerricher State Park Rd. **Trailhead GPS: N39 27.487' / W123 48.469'**

The Georgia Pacific Haul Road Bridge spans the Noyo River downstream of Newman Gulch, about 1.3 miles east of downtown. **Trailhead GPS: N39 26.031' / W123 47.228'**

Green Acres Campground and RV Park is located at 23600 N. Hwy. 1, just north of Fort Bragg. Its phone number is (707) 964-1425. **Campground GPS: N39 29.010' / W123 47.718'**

4

The Watchers

Mendocino Woodlands State Park, Manly Gulch Trail
Mendocino, Mendocino County

TORIES ABOUT UNKNOWN dangers lurking deep within the forest go as far back as anyone can remember. The fears, not totally unfounded, form the basis of many popular fairy tales, such as Hansel and Gretel, Little Red Riding Hood, and Snow White.

So no one should scoff at hikers who claim that the unblinking eyes of unseen beings peer out at them from behind the trees in Mendocino Woodlands State Park. Located on the Northern California coast 10 miles south of Fort Bragg and 7 miles east of the town of Mendocino, the park is situated along the Little North Fork of the Big River in the heart of redwood country. There are approximately 25 miles of hiking trails in and around the park, and some of them also wind through the adjoining Jackson State Forest.

When first set aside, the forest reserve had more than 5,000 acres. One of forty-six campgrounds built in the 1930s by the Works Progress Administration and the Civilian Conservation Corps as "Recreation Demonstration Areas" was located there. The camp's original purpose was to give city kids a chance to experience nature, but the forest has always been a popular camping site for young and old alike.

The site was downsized to its present 700 acres when it became Mendocino Woodlands State Park in 1976 and is administered by the

California Department of Forestry. The park is listed on the US National Register of Historic Places and is a US National Historic Landmark.

There have been accounts of eerie shadowy, human-shaped figures in the forest, silent sentinels staring out at park visitors. Some folks believe the apparitions are simply squatters living in the woods, but many nearby residents call them the "watchers." If locals discuss the spirits at all, they say that whoever the people were, they are long dead. Nothing has been able to get rid of the ghosts.

One old wives' tale says that, when alive, the spectres were drunken drifters who were murdered by gang members as part of an initiation rite. Could the phantoms be peeking out at hikers in the hopes that someday they'll spot their murderers and be able to take revenge? Fortunately, there have been no stories about the ghosts confronting anyone on the trail— yet! But it *has* been said that the spooks do sometimes follow people home.

Haunted Trails

The most haunted hike in Mendocino Woodlands State Park seems to be the Manley Gulch Trail. The path is in a ravine located between the Mendocino Woodlands Outdoor Center to the southwest and Thompson Gulch to the northeast. The trail is a 4.2-mile out-and-back path that's rated moderate, even though it descends about 900 feet into the gorge. From the bottom of the canyon, which is flat, trails branch off in several directions if you want to extend your hike.

Manley Gulch Trail is lightly traveled, normally quiet and serene. It's a beautiful stroll through second-growth redwood and other flora. Be aware, though, that it's also a bike trail, and cyclists can come up on you suddenly from behind. The trail starts off Little Lake Road (FR 408). The turnaround point of the hike is at Camp Road on the floor of the ravine. The trail is open year-round. **Trailhead GPS: N39 20.390' / W123 43.244'**

For updates on Mendocino Woodlands State Park, including open hours, call (707) 937-5755. For information about a 5-mile hike that starts on the old logging road through Thompson Gulch and ends with the ascent up Manley Gulch Trail, check out https://mendowalks.org/JSDF/index.php?i=5. Both trailheads are on Little Lake Road.

The Cascades, the Sierra Nevada, and Death Valley

1 Mount Shasta
Shasta-Trinity National Forest

2 Lassen National Forest

3 Bumpass Hell Trail, Cold Boiling Lake Trail
Lassen Volcanic National Park

4 The Downieville Downhill, Sunrise Trail
Downieville

5 Donner Memorial State Park, Donner Lake
Truckee

6 Tahoe Rim Trail, Pacific Crest Trail,
Tahoe National Forest

7 Crystal Basin
Eldorado National Forest

8 Hidden Falls Regional Park,
Hidden Falls Access Trail,
Blue Oak Loop, Creek Side Trail
to Great Egret Trail Loop,
Hidden Falls Trail to River Otter Loop,
South Legacy Way
Auburn

9 Sailor Bar
Fair Oaks

10 Utica Reservoir
Stanislaus National Forest

11 Arnold Rim Trail, Stanislaus
National Forest
Arnold

12 Chilnualna Falls Trail, Bridalveil
Fall Trail, Tenaya Canyon
Yosemite National Park

13 Dry Creek Running Trail
Modesto

14 Coldwater Campground, Lake George
Campground, Lake Mary Campground,
Mammoth Mountain RV Park, McGee Creek
RV Park and Campground, New Shady Rest
Campground, Old Shady Rest Campground,
Pine Glen Group Campground,
Sherwin Creek Campground, Twin Lakes
Mammoth Lakes

15 Doris Lake, Florence Lake, Mono, Old Pedro,
Evolution Valley, Range of Light, Mono Hot
Springs Campgrounds, Old Pedro,
Hot Springs Resort cabins, post office, and cafe
Mono Hot Springs

16 High Sierra Trail, Giant Forest Loop Trail,
Moro Rock, Crystal Cave
Sequoia National Park

17 Barker Ranch, Wingate Pass, Hells Gate,
Racetrack Playa, Skidoo, Amargosa
Opera House and Hotel
Death Valley National Park

5

The Underground City

Mount Shasta
Shasta-Trinity National Forest, Shasta County

MOUNT SHASTA HAS been the subject of paranormal legends seemingly forever. The most common claim is that there's an ancient hidden city beneath the mighty peak. The mountain stands at 14,179 feet, close to the Oregon border at the southern end of the Cascade Range. A dormant volcano, Shasta may have erupted as recently as two centuries ago, and most volcanologists, including those at the US Geological Survey, consider it to be potentially active. (Research has shown that over the last 10,000 years, the mountain has erupted every 600 to 800 years.)

It's possible that early Spanish explorers may have sighted Mount Shasta, but the first non–Native American to report it was Peter Skene Ogden, who saw it while working for the Hudson Bay Company. He mentioned the mountain in his 1926–27 journal, calling it "Sastise" for a local tribe. Over time the moniker morphed into "Shasta," and it officially became the mountain's name in 1841. (As a side note, current historians believe Ogden may have actually been referring to a different peak.)

The mountain has inspired poets, writers, and artists for generations. Klamath folklore says that Skell, the Spirit of the Above-World, inhabits the peak. In one legend, a chieftain called on Skell to fight Llao, the Spirit of the Below-World, who lived in Mount Mazama. In a series of epic battles, they tossed lava and scalding rocks at each other from their respective mountaintops. Is it possible that volcanic eruptions seen by the area's earliest inhabitants formed the basis for these venerable beliefs?

Legends persist that there's a secret hidden city somewhere inside Mount Shasta. The myth dates back to at least 1899, with the publication of Frederick Spencer Oliver's book, *A Dweller on Two Planets*. In it, he claimed that back in prehistory there was a technologically advanced race of people who lived on a now-lost continent called Lemuria. In a giant geological upheaval, the landmass sank and became submerged beneath the ocean. Some of its inhabitants managed to escape and made their way to Mount Shasta. The Lemurians constructed Telos, a vast city inside the sleeping volcano, as well as an extensive system of tunnels. Oliver also claimed that, even in his day, Lemurians, dressed in long white robes, could occasionally be spotted on the slopes of Mount Shasta.

The tale reached a new audience in 1931 when the Rosicrucians published a book by Harvey Spencer Lewis about Mount Shasta and the Lemurians. Also in the early '30s, a mystic named Guy Ballard founded the "I AM" Movement, a metaphysical religion closely related to theosophy. He said he had been instructed by a mysterious man he encountered while hiking on Mount Shasta. Ballard maintained that the stranger identified himself as St. Germain, a major figure in theosophical teachings.

Many, if not all, of these strange narratives have since been interwoven and incorporated into occult religions and New Age thought.

For those who prefer more secular stories, a British prospector named J. C. Brown announced he discovered an underground city in Mount Shasta in 1904 after following a descending tunnel from the surface for 11 miles. Although he didn't encounter any living beings, much less Lemurians, Brown allegedly found gold, warriors' shields, and several mummies—some of them 10 feet tall! For better or worse, he left everything in place when he emerged, so he had nothing to prove his wild tale. In 1934 an expedition was mounted in Stockton to search for the tunnel. Brown was supposed to lead the undertaking, but on the morning it was to set out, he never showed up.

If you hike anywhere on Mount Shasta and discover the gateway to Telos, you'll be hailed as a real-life, modern-day Indiana Jones. Dust off that weathered fedora!

According to a popular old wives' tale, the hazy spectre of a young woman silently crying appears every Halloween—and only on Halloween—in one of the campgrounds along a river in Shasta-Trinity National Forest. Campers usually spot her standing on the shore, but she occasionally walks out onto the water as well. It's said that many years ago, she fell into the river and drowned. The unknown woman's ghost has returned because she felt she didn't deserve to die and had unfinished business. She normally keeps her distance from the living, but she'll push people out of her way if they block her path. It's said that if she passes out of sight and you follow her, you'll never come back.

It's notable that no particular body of water is ever mentioned in this legend. Such stories have a tendency to be light on details to begin with, and then, by the time they get passed down from one generation to the next, what few specifics there were become forgotten or confused.

For example, four rivers pass through Shasta-Trinity National Forest: Trinity River, McCloud River, Pit River, and even a short arm of the Sacramento River. In addition to these major waterways, there are numerous creeks as well—in all, 6,278 miles of streams and rivers. Then there are the hundreds of mountain lakes. Almost all of the waterways have established campgrounds or sites for individual camping somewhere alongside. So who knows where these annual hauntings supposedly take place, if at all.

Haunted Trails

The first recorded successful ascent of Mount Shasta was in 1854. These days there's an established alpine-style route that starts in Avalanche Gulch. Almost all of Mount Shasta's climbers take this path. The ascent is described as "aggressive and challenging" and should only be undertaken by people who have had the proper training and are in very good physical condition. For practiced mountaineers, it generally takes two or three days. The 6-mile West Face route begins at the Bunny Flat trailhead. **Trailhead GPS: N41 21.243' / W122 14.013'**

An alternate path to the summit, also requiring mountaineering expertise, is the 5-mile Hotlum-Bolan Ridge climb that starts at the North Gate trailhead. **Trailhead GPS: N41 28.099' / W122 19.429'**

Before making any attempt to climb to the top of Mount Shasta, you should check first with the USDA Forest Service (fs.usda.gov/Internet/ FSE_DOCUMENTS/fsm9_008138.pdf) and ShastaGuides.com for current conditions and their recommendations. And don't forget to tell someone where you're going!

Of course, you don't have to go to the peak of the mountain to enjoy Shasta-Trinity National Forest. Numerous trails of various lengths can be found on and around the base of Mount Shasta, from short, easy hikes to those of moderate or hard difficulty. You can find listings online at visitmtshasta.com/activities/hiking-backpacking/ and at alltrails.com/us/ california/mount-shasta, among several other places.

6

The Spirit Orbs

Bumpass Hell Trail, Cold Boiling Lake Trail
Lassen Volcanic National Park, Shasta, Lassen, Plumas, and
Tehama Counties

Lassen National Forest
Lassen County

LASSEN PEAK AND Cinder Cone, two natural wonders in north-eastern California, were designated national monuments by President Theodore Roosevelt in 1907. Eight years later, Lassen Volcanic National Park was established with 100,000 acres surrounding the domes.

Standing at 10,460 feet, Lassen Peak is the largest plug dome volcano in the world. It's also the southernmost nonextinct volcano in the Cascade Range. The peak is named for Peter Lassen, a local miner and rancher who promoted the area to pioneers coming west over the Cascades in the 1830s. The landmark was a signpost for settlers to turn south toward the fertile Sacramento Valley.

As its name suggests, Cinder Cone is a cinder cone volcano, and it's located about 10 miles southeast of Lassen Peak. It was once thought the cone erupted as recently as 1851, but volcanologists now believe it's been dormant since 1666.

The last recorded eruption anywhere in Lassen Volcanic National Park took place in 1917, and much of the land remains active geothermally. It's dotted with sulfurous steam vents, hot springs, geysers, mud pots, and dormant volcanoes. The park also contains lakes, streams, glacier-cut canyons, and numerous permanent snowfields. For hiking enthusiasts, it has more than 150 miles of trails.

Abutting Lassen Volcanic National Park to the east is the 1,700-square-mile Lassen National Forest, which was founded in 1905. It, too, contains volcanic cones and craters and even an underground lava tube called Subway Cave. The forest's main attractions, however, are its sparkling lakes, waterfalls, ravines, buttes, meadows, and endless recreational trails.

Approximately 64 miles of the Pacific Crest Trail, which stretches 2,650 miles from Mexico to Canada, run through Lassen Volcanic National Park and Lassen National Forest. Elevations on the trail range from 3,200 to 5,500 feet as it passes along mountain ridges, through wooded areas, and across open fields. Some sections are covered with snow until late spring. All experienced backpackers have heard of the PCT, so they know that hiking the Lassen portion should not be undertaken as a spur-of-the-moment day trip.

There are dozens of other equally scenic treks in Lassen Volcanic National Park. If there is anything that could be called a "must-do" for visitors, it's a descent into Bumpass Hell, the park's most spectacular geothermal region. (Other popular thermal areas include Boiling Springs Lake, Devils Kitchen, Little Hot Springs Valley, and Sulphur Works.)

Bumpass Hell encompasses 16 acres of active fumaroles, hissing vents, bubbling mud, and boiling pools. It was named for Kendall Vanhook Bumpass, a local resident. He was leading a group through the basin in 1865 when one of his feet broke through the brittle, thin crust of what looked like solid ground. His leg plunged into a boiling mud pot, severely scalding it and requiring amputation. Today you can walk through Bumpass Hell safely via a marked plank path.

Both the Lassen Volcanic National Park and the Lassen National Forest are home to strange floating orbs of yellow light. If the glowing spheres only appeared in the geothermal areas, they could, perhaps, be explained as sulfurous gas clouds hovering over the open, heated pools. But, no, they're also seen flitting through the trees and above open fields and streams.

Spotting the spooky spheres is unnerving enough, but the orbs are sometimes dangerous. Usually it's impossible to catch one of them, as they always seem to be just out of reach. But there have been a few reports of people who succeeded in touching them, and as their fingers made contact—and sometimes just before—they fell into seizures.

The orbs seen at Lassen are uniformly yellow, but similar spheres appear throughout the world in a variety of colors. Some paranormalists suggest that each color has a specific meaning, and yellow is most often interpreted as being a warning or bad omen. Until we know for certain what the unearthly orbs are, beware. Look, but don't touch!

Scientists tend to discount such balls of light as swamp gas, light refraction, or illuminated dust particles. In ghost lore, however, it's believed that these orbs could be manifestations of deceased individuals who have returned from the Other Side or are trapped here on the Mortal Plane.

Haunted Trails

Bumpass Hell is an easy 3-mile, heavily trafficked out-and-back path. The trailhead is at one end of a parking area on Lassen Peak Highway. **Trailhead GPS: N40 27.961' / W121 130.847'**

The trail provides one photo opportunity after another. Shortly after starting out, there's a tremendous view of the distant Lassen Peak reflected in Lake Helen. **Photo Outlook GPS: N40 27.985' / W121 30.665'**

After another 0.5 mile or so on the trail, an overlook allows you to peer across a deep valley to Brokeoff and Diller Mountains. As you approach Bumpass Hell itself, you'll crest a small hill. From the top, you'll get your first glimpse of the eerie, almost indescribable terrain. You'll also know you're getting close when you hear the sound of gurgling water and smell the scent of sulfur wafting through the air. A sturdy, railed board-walk allows you to get close to all of the action.

Bumpass Hell Basin can also be accessed from Cold Boiling Lake Trail. A short turnoff from Lassen Peak Highway takes you to the trail-head, where there is limited parking. **Trailhead GPS: N40 27.596' / W121 28.456'**

The hike to the lake from this direction is a 1.4-mile out-and-back trail of moderate difficulty with moderate traffic. From Cold Boiling Lake, you can connect with the far side of Bumpass Hell Trail and follow it to the basin.

You can check out a short video about Bumpass Hell Trail on the National Park Service website at nps.gov/lavo/planyourvisit/hiking_bumpass_hell.htm.

When planning your visit, remember that Lassen National Volcanic Park and Lassen National Forest are in mountainous territory. Roads and trails are subject to closure due to snow in the winter and spring. July to October is the best time to visit.

7

Terror in Truckee

Donner Memorial State Park, Donner Lake
Truckee, Nevada County

The Downieville Downhill, Sunrise Trail
Downieville, Sierra County

THE DONNER PARTY—THREE words that send a chill up the spine of anyone who's even vaguely familiar with the band's tragic struggle to cross the Sierra Nevada and the gruesome decision some of them were forced to make to stay alive.

In the spring of 1846, George Donner, James F. Reed, their extended families, and several employees set out from Independence, Missouri, in nine wagons, heading westward in search of a new life. In June they caught up to a larger wagon train on the way to Fort Laramie, Wyoming, and joined it.

The route to California from Fort Laramie was well established. Settlers would travel the Oregon Trail to Fort Hall on the Snake River, which is in present-day Idaho. From there, they would either travel through Oregon then turn south, or they would take the more difficult but shorter California Trail that cut across northern Nevada.

There were other routes to California being discovered as well, some better than others. Unfortunately, the Donners, Reeds, and several other families decided to split from the main caravan to take a shortcut: an untried route that Lansford Hastings, a California land promoter, had briefly mentioned in his 1845 book *The Emigrants' Guide to Oregon and California*. He claimed that by traveling southwest over the Wasatch Mountains and crossing the Great Salt Lake Basin, pioneers could save 350 miles on their journey. Theoretically, that was true, but Hastings didn't bother to mention that neither he nor anyone else had ever attempted to make the passage with fully laden ox-drawn wagons.

The breakaway party, with more than eighty souls traveling in sixty to eighty wagons, chose Donner as their leader. According to some sources, the group expected to meet Hastings along the way, thinking that he would guide them over the mountains. But Hastings never showed.

Entire books have been written on the hardships the Donner party endured over the next several months. First, the trail over the Wasatch Mountains was very primitive and overgrown; the company had to clear much of it themselves. Water and food were scarce once they entered the Great Salt Lake Desert, and wagon wheels sank into the sandy, crusted soil, slowing them down. Their route eventually joined the existing California Trail at the Humboldt River, but by then several of the pioneers had already died. Taking the so-called Hastings Cutoff had cost the Donner party an extra month.

They reached the eastern slope of the Sierra Nevada by late October, much later in the season than most wagon trains. They had been told that snow wouldn't block the Fremont Pass (now Donner Pass) at the summit until mid-November, so they decided to take their chances. What could be worse than what they had already experienced? And once they were on the other side of the mountains, they would be in California.

Of course, everything went wrong. The climb was much steeper than they anticipated, and then an early snow began to fall. By the time the first six families made it to Truckee Lake (now Donner Lake), the pass was, well, impassable. Days went by. After many attempts to make it through the pass, the party realized it was futile. They had to set up camp for the winter.

There was an empty cabin near the lake that had been built two years earlier by another California-bound settler, Moses Schallenberger. The Breen family—presumably the first arrivals from the Donner party— moved in. The Murphys built a new cabin backed against a gigantic boulder for protection from the wind, and a third cabin was built for the Graves and Reed families. In all, sixty people divvied up the three small dirt-floor pine cabins. They had no windows and used buffalo or ox hides for roofs.

Members of the Donner family itself were among the last to arrive. One of their wagons had broken an axle on the ascent, which took several days to repair. When they finally reached the summit, they set up shelter next to Alder Creek, about 7 miles from the cabins.

There was little food left at the encampment. A few fish were caught in the lake and streams before they froze over. One bear was killed. Soon the horses and oxen, already emaciated, began to die. Once their meat was consumed, the snowbound settlers were forced to eat jellied ox hide. The animals' bones were boiled repeatedly to make soup. The pioneers were so desperate they even roasted and ate the ox hide rugs that were covering the floors.

Before long, the trapped pioneers began to die from malnutrition, starvation, the frigid weather, or disease. With little hope left, seventeen men, women, and children, led by William Eddy, set out on foot to try to breach the pass. History books now refer to them as the Forlorn Hope. Three people soon turned back to the camp at Donner Lake, but the others pressed on. One man paused to rest and told the others to keep going: He would catch up. His remains were found the following year.

By the eighth day out, Christmas Eve, all of the food the Forlorn Hope had brought with them was gone, and they were too tired to continue. They realized—as unthinkable as it might be—that cannibalism was the only way they would be able to survive. Over the next week, five members of the party died. Most of their meat was devoured immediately, but some was cured for later consumption.

Up to that point, no one had been killed for food, but two Indian guides who had refused to devour human flesh began to fear for their lives. One night, they secretly left camp and set out on their own. When the others caught up to them a few days later, the Native Americans were close to death. They had not eaten in more than a week. One of the trekkers, William Foster, knowing the inevitable, took it upon himself to shoot the men to hasten their demise. Eddy was so angry and appalled by the murder that he felt he could no longer continue to travel with Foster. The group split up, some trusting Eddy to save them, the others staying with Foster.

Eddy and those who followed him staggered into a Native American camp on January 12, 1847. It had taken them thirty-three days to make it from Donner Lake to safety. Five days later the company reached another native village, where a member of the tribe agreed to lead the ragged group to Sutter's Fort, a trading garrison owned by John Sutter (on whose mill gold would be discovered the following year).

Back in October, James Reed had been banished from the Donner party for killing another man during an argument. Traveling alone on horseback, Reed had been able to beat the snow and reached Sutter's Fort by the end of the month. His family had been allowed to stay with the wagon caravan, however, and as weeks went by with no sign of them, Reed became more and more worried.

When Eddy arrived at the trading post and told his story, Reed immediately called for a rescue party to be formed. Starting out on his own, Reed managed to find Foster and his group, which by then had crossed the pass. A relief group of seven men reached the cabins at Donner Lake on February 18. Two more rescue teams followed.

Incredibly, Tamsen Donner chose not to leave with the last group, even though she knew that no others would come until spring. She remained behind to comfort and care for her husband, George, who had slashed his hand while repairing the family's wagon back in October and lay dying of gangrene. After George's death in early April, Tamsen decided to try to cross the pass but only made it as far as the Murphy cabin, where she passed away. Both the rescue teams and a later salvage party found evidence that some of the people trapped at the summit had turned to cannibalism, just like the Forlorn Hope group.

According to most historians, there were eighty-seven people in the Donner party when it started up the Wasatch Mountains. Only forty-eight made it alive to California.

In 1918 a statue of a pioneer family was erected on the former site of the Schallenberger-Breen cabin as a reminder of the tragic events of 1846–47. The bronze stands on top of a 22-foot pedestal, said to have been the depth of the snow at the summit that winter. In 1928 the State of California established Donner Memorial State Park on 11 acres surrounding the monument. The grounds were expanded in 1947 to include the former location of the Murphy cabin. The statue and old cabin site were named National Historic Landmarks in 1963. A new visitor center and museum located near the Pioneer Monument opened in 2015.

Donner Memorial State Park is located in Truckee, just west of downtown and about 15 miles north of Lake Tahoe. It abuts the eastern edge of Donner Lake and wraps partway around its southern shore. The 3,293-acre park offers more than 8 miles of hiking and snow trails.

Nighttime visitors to the park sometimes catch sight of a female apparition floating over the grounds, bathed in a shimmering amber aura. According to legend, the spirit is Tamsen Donner. Your best chance to run into her is on one of the park trails near the Murphy cabin site.

Many visitors to Donner Lake have spotted an unusual beast with sharp, jagged teeth and webbed hands swimming beneath the surface of the water. But it's not a ghost. Folklore suggests that the unnamed creature was once human, a drowning victim in the lake. Somehow, it has morphed into the monster that's spied today. Be careful when swimming there: It's said that the amphibious fiend is looking for a mate!

It's hard to imagine what it would have been like trying to cross the Sierra Nevada before there were any roads—*and* in wintertime! Today,

I-80 makes it an easy journey, even though snow conditions temporarily close portions of the highway from time to time. The interstate passes just north of the true Donner Pass, which is located between the community of Norden and the Donner Summit Bridge on a section of the old US 40.

Downieville, also located in the Tahoe National Forest but across the Sierra County line, is about 60 miles northwest of Truckee by car or 30 miles as the crow flies—not that such a direct route exists. The community lies at the confluence of the Downie and Yuba Rivers and was founded in 1849 when gold was discovered nearby. Although small—the town has only a few hundred year-round residents—it's a popular base for hiking, fishing, kayaking, off-road motor sports, and mountain biking.

The area biking trails are rumored to be haunted by an evil entity that likes to attack the living, especially women and girls. Many female hikers have reported feeling uneasy on the trails, and invisible hands have tried to grasp some of them from behind. Several of the near-victims later discovered fingernail scratches on their bodies where they had been touched. The identity of the malevolent spirit is unknown.

Haunted Trails

Donner Lake Ridge Trail
The Donner Lake Ridge Trail isn't on the shoreline: It follows the crests of the hills from west to east overlooking the northern side of the lake. The hike is 15.6 miles out and back from the Castle Valley Access trailhead, which is located at exit 176 of I-80. **Trailhead GPS: N39 20.449' / W120 20.857'**

Donner Lake Ridge Trail can also be accessed via the 0.8-mile unpaved Glacier Way Access Trail, which has a parking area at its trailhead. **Trailhead GPS: N39 20.591' / W120 16.104'**

Donner Lake Ridge Trail is part of a proposed 23-mile path that will completely encircle the lake. About 5 miles of the already-existing Pacific

Crest Trail would be incorporated into the route on the west side of the lake.

Several possible routes on the south side of the lake are being considered for the trail to link up with Donner Lake Ridge Trail, but a 10.5-mile moderately trafficked route of moderate difficulty already exists. Almost all of it lies within Donner Memorial State Park. Known as the Schallenberger Ridge, Emigrant Canyon and Coldstream Loop, the pathway offers remarkable views of Donner Lake and the environs. Check at the visitor center before setting off. There have been reports that sections of the trail are not well marked. **Trailhead GPS: N39 19.120' / W120 13.875'**

Downieville Downhill

The Downieville Downhill is the most popular local trail in the Downieville area, and it's a classic downhill biking path. Riders are shuttled from town to the top of the track near Packer Lake Saddle. From there, it's 14 to 16 miles down the mountainside, crossing bridges, creeks, and rocks and passing by swimming holes and waterfalls. Eighty-five to 90 percent of the ride is a singletrack, and it has an overall intermediate to difficult rating. Surveys regularly list it as one of the top singletrack trails in the West. **Trailhead GPS: N39 37.162' / W120 40.031'**

If you're traveling by foot and want just a taste of the Downieville Downhill, try the first section of the path, which is known as Sunrise Trail. It's just shy of 2 miles long and is of moderate difficulty. It stretches from the shuttle drop-off point to the Butcher Ranch trailhead. **Trailhead GPS: N39 37.172' / W120 40.998'**

More precise information as well as shuttle reservations can be obtained at Yuba Expeditions in downtown Downieville (530-289-3010; yubaexpeditions.com).

8

The Hunchback Horror

Tahoe Rim Trail, Pacific Crest Trail
Tahoe National Forest, Placer County

Crystal Basin
Eldorado National Forest, El Dorado County

I T DOESN'T TAKE much to fall in love with Lake Tahoe. Located at an elevation of 6,225 feet in the Sierra Nevada, it's the largest alpine lake in North America. The only deeper lake in the United States is Oregon's Crater Lake, and the only bigger American lakes by volume are the Great Lakes. Lake Tahoe (often simply referred to as Tahoe) lies on the California-Nevada border, with about two-thirds of the shoreline in the former state.

Prior to pioneer migration from the East, the Washoe Native Americans inhabited the area. The first outsider to see the lake was Lt. John C. Fremont, who spotted it during his expedition of 1844. The US Department of Interior began calling it Tahoe (from the Washoe word meaning "lake") in 1862. The name didn't become official, though, until 1945!

Prospectors passed through the region in 1848 during the California gold rush; more followed after the discovery of the Comstock Lode in Nevada. Logging became Tahoe's first major industry, but tourism wasn't far behind. Tahoe City was founded in California on the lake's northern shore in 1864 as a resort for residents of Virginia City, Nevada. Regular train service to the lake soon began, along with steamboat transportation on the water. As roads were improved, the mountain getaway became easily accessible by car.

The lake, surrounding forests, and mountain slopes have made Tahoe a popular year-round destination. Spring through autumn brings hikers, swimmers, boaters, and divers; snow attracts skiers and enthusiasts of other winter recreational activities. And ever since Nevada legalized gambling in 1931, casinos have drawn visitors to the south shore.

Hikes in Tahoe National Forest and near the lake are exhilarating, and usually they're pretty tranquil. That is, unless you run into the notorious hunchbacked creature that roams its trails.

The beast is certainly not human. Everyone who's seen it has described it as dark, massive, and sinister. And, of course, there's that ever-present hump. This isn't ancient folklore we're talking about. Sightings in the Lake Tahoe Basin have been reported in the *Union* newspaper and aired on Fox News as recently as 2014. Surprisingly, the being hasn't yet been given a name or even a nickname.

Usually when the creepy creature is spotted, it's crouched close to the ground. At first glance, some folks think it's digging for something, although no one has seen it carrying anything away. The unidentified animal has been known to jump onto trails directly in front of backpackers and bikers, blocking their way. And the beast will lurch at anyone foolish enough to approach it. A few hikers—a *very* few—have reported being attacked by the creature, but their claims have never been backed up by photos of the injuries or medical records. So far, everyone who's encountered the hideous hunchback has lived to tell the tale.

Even those who haven't seen the entity occasionally hear its howls and shrieks coming from inside the forest, especially at night. Sightings are more common when the weather is warm, but that could simply be because there are fewer hikers on the trails in the winter.

So does this mysterious humanoid actually exist? It's not any known species. Nor is it a Sasquatch. But it definitely falls into the category of

Tahoe Rim Trail, Lake Tahoe.
PHOTO COURTESY OF KENT ERVIN

legendary creatures known as crytpids. Studied by cryptozoologists, these are animals whose existence is based solely on anecdotal evidence or old wives' tales rather than scientific proof. Examples of fellow cryptids are Bigfoot, the Loch Ness Monster, Mothman, and the chupacabra.

And surely *those* exist.

Crystal Basin contains about 85,000 acres of the Eldorado National Forest southwest of Lake Tahoe. The distinct geological region has five lakes, the largest of which is Union Valley Reservoir, with 20 miles of shoreline. Recreational activities in the area include camping, fishing, boating, cross-country skiing, horseback riding, mountain biking, and, of course, hiking.

The ghost of a man wearing an early to mid-twentieth-century suit roams Crystal Basin at night, silently passing from one campground to the next. The unknown apparition hasn't hurt anyone—so far—but some people have woken up in their tents to see the phantom standing over them with a knife in his hand. Rather than attacking, the spectre disappears the instant it's spotted.

Haunted Trails

The best-known hiking path at Lake Tahoe is the 169.3-mile Tahoe Rim Trail (TRT) that encircles the lake. Traffic varies from one section to the next. Although some parts are easier than others, the trail is rated to be of hard difficulty overall. Even if you don't tackle the entire perimeter, walking just a few miles anywhere along this route is immensely rewarding. If you're up for the whole expedition, plan to spend about thirteen days. Bear in mind that only experienced backpackers should attempt the entire trek. You can start the hike at any spot on the trail, of course, but the traditional trailhead is on the Nevada side of the lake. **Trailhead GPS: N39 06.263' / W119 53.833'**

The path can also be joined easily in Tahoe City, one of the few places the TRT descends to the shoreline. **Trailhead GPS: N39 10.155' / W120 08.927'**

9

The Chimeric Children

Hidden Falls Regional Park, Hidden Falls Access Trail, Blue Oak Loop, Creek Side Trail to Great Egret Trail Loop, Hidden Falls Trail to River Otter Loop, South Legacy Way
Auburn, Placer County

Sailor Bar
Fair Oaks, Sacramento County

EVERYONE HAS HEARD the old adage that the shortest distance between two points is a straight line. What the maxim doesn't say is that sticking to the path is also often safest. There are countless stories in folklore about ghosts, magical beings, and evil creatures luring people away from their tasks at hand, only to bewitch, capture, or kill them. Of course, that sort of thing only happens in fairy tales. Doesn't it?

Hidden Falls Regional Park, which opened in 2006, is located north of Sacramento, just 5 miles west of CA 49 in Placer County. Its name suggests that the recreational area is "hidden" in the Sierra foothills between Auburn and Lincoln. Gold was found in nearby Auburn Ravine in May 1848, and, before long, prospectors and mining companies had forced out the Nisenan Native Americans who were living there.

In 1865 the town of Auburn linked up with the transcontinental railroad, and the region's clement weather, plentiful water, and large open spaces drew hundreds of fruit farmers and ranchers. In time Hidden Falls Regional Park was able to expand to its present size in 2013 by acquiring land from adjacent former ranches. The park now spans 1,200 acres, but its most traversed trails are found in its original 220 acres.

Be on the lookout while hiking anywhere in the park. You may run into spectral children along the way. No one knows who the youngsters could be—or were. Their general appearance gives us few clues, except that their clothing seems to be from the twentieth rather than the nine-teenth century. There are no records of a group of children dying or being buried in the area, so there's not even a historical explanation as to why their spirits have chosen to return to the site—much less why they have become so sinister.

You're most likely to run into these otherworldly urchins during the warmest months of the year, especially when wildflowers are in bloom. It can happen anywhere in the park, but the spectres are most often encoun-tered standing back a bit from one of the established trails. The impish phantoms appear to be flesh and blood, and they certainly seem innocent enough. At least, at first.

They call to you, imploring you to follow them into the woods, claim-ing they want to show you a spectacular waterfall they've discovered. They say you'll never find it on your own because it's not on any map or trail guide. It's a secret set of falls, and only they know how to get to it.

Whatever you do, don't follow them! And as soon as you turn down their seemingly innocent request, run! Otherwise, you'll see their moods darken and the sweet smiles leave their faces. They may decide to chase after you, taunting you with hideous threats and macabre laughter. But if you keep moving, they won't catch up.

The spirited spooks sometimes employ a different tactic to snare you. They hide behind the trees bordering a trail and wait. Eventually, the sound of the unseen children giggling and playing will stop some unsus-pecting passerby. Curious, he or she will wander into the forest to find the noises' source. If you hear this "siren song," don't leave the trail. It's a trap!

What happens to those who can't resist, wander into the woods, or follow them away from the path? Does the hidden waterfall even exist? No one knows. No backpacker that's gone with the phantoms has ever come back. Sometimes it's better not to stop and smell the roses!

Fair Oaks is located 38 miles southwest of Auburn on the banks of the American River. One of the town's chief recreational areas is Sailor Bar Park on the waterfront. Its name comes from an apocryphal tale that a sailor (whose identity has been lost in time) jumped ship in San Francisco during the California gold rush. He traveled inland up the American River, staked claims on a river bar at what is today Fair Oaks, and successfully panned for gold. Later, the search for gold was mechanized: Now on just about any hike in Sailor Bar Park, you'll pass dredge tailings left behind from when gold was mined there from the 1850s to the 1940s.

The 114-acre city park is on the north shore of the American River and extends from Hazel Bridge to the east to Fair Oaks Bluff (near the intersection of Olive and Natoma Avenues) to the west. Although some parts of the park are barren, much of it is covered with green fields, wildflowers in season, and oak trees. Numerous trails traverse Sailor Bar Park. Many of them are dirt paths, some are gravel service roads, but all of them are gated and hike-in only. The trails are popular with backpackers, bird-watchers, bicyclists, and equestrians. Dogs are allowed too. There's also a boat launch from a cul-de-sac at the southern end of Illinois Avenue.

A male ghost walks up to hikers on the trails but vanishes before getting too close. To many, the spectre's clothing looks like fishing attire, and it's always soaked, so it's thought that the unknown man was a drowning victim in the river. At least one ranger has seen the phantom while locking up a park restroom at night.

Haunted Trails

Hidden Falls Regional Park

Hidden Falls Regional Park has about 30 miles of paths, 30-foot water-falls, observation decks, bridges, benches, and multiple access points to Coon Creek, which runs through the park.

The most popular pathway in the park is Hidden Falls Trail, a 3.2-mile loop trail of moderate difficulty. On busy days, you'll have lots of company. **Trailhead GPS: N38 57.547' / W121 09.839'**

Blue Oak Loop Trail is an easy, forested 3.2-mile loop trail. **Trailhead GPS: N38 56.543' / W121 09.827'**

Creek Side Trail to Great Egret Trail Loop is an 8.5-mile loop trail of moderate difficulty with an overlook of the falls. There are many tempting forks off this trail. **Trailhead GPS: N38 57.510' / W121 09.843'**

The Hidden Falls to River Otter Loop is an easy 4.2-mile trail that offers a waterfall view. **Trailhead GPS: N38 57.528' / W121 09.853'**

South Legacy Way, a 4.2-mile out-and-back trail, is of moderate difficulty and features a waterfall view along the way. **Trailhead GPS: N38 57.545' / W121 09.843'**

Many of the park's paths intersect or branch off of one another, so it's possible to hike many of them in just a few hours. Dogs are allowed but must be leashed. If you prefer riding to walking, bicycles and horses are permitted on the paths, but access is often restricted during and after heavy rain. Due to limited parking, a guaranteed reservation is required to enter Hidden Falls Regional Park on weekends and holidays. Reservations are not issued on-site and must be made online in advance. For more information, visit https://www.placer.ca.gov/6106/Hidden-Falls-Regional-Park.

The park's major hiking paths are signposted with maps at their trail-heads. If your main interest is seeing the waterfalls and you want to avoid crowds, hike very early or late in the day, especially on weekends.

Sailor Bar

The many trails on Sailor Bar are mostly level with little change in elevation, so all of the park's hikes are of easy difficulty. Depending upon how much you meander around Sailor Bar, it's possible to walk several miles with little effort. Multiple paths set out from the second parking lot you come to after entering the park via Illinois Avenue. One trail heads north into a Nature Study Area that has a pond. Another trail goes west and stretches along part of the northern boundary of the park. There are also paths from the lot that head eastward or south toward the river. **Parking Lot GPS: N38 38.278' / W121 14.235'**

The western access to Sailor Bar Park is Olive Avenue, and the street leads to two adjacent parking lots for vehicles. Two main trails depart from the lots, and both are gated to vehicular traffic. One of the paths, actually a continuation of Olive Avenue, travels east and transverses the park. **Trailhead GPS: N38 38.417' / W121 15.210'**

The second trail also sets out from the Olive Avenue parking area. It heads south but soon turns eastward to follow the American River. **Trailhead GPS: N38 38.385' / W121 15.265'**

To get to Sailor Bar Park from US 50, exit onto Hazel Avenue and travel north, crossing the river. Turn left at Winding Way and left again onto Illinois Avenue. The park entrance on Illinois will be at the bottom of a small hill. The park is open daily from sunrise to sunset. There is a fee for parking, with no weekend or holiday exceptions. Payment is made at self-serve kiosks. Be sure to display the payment stub or receipt on your vehicle's dashboard before you begin your hike. For more information, call (916) 875-6961 or check out https://regionalparks.saccounty.net/Parks/Pages/SailorBar.aspx. The site has a link to a simple trail map.

10

The Stanislaus Siren

Arnold Rim Trail, Stanislaus National Forest
Arnold, Calaveras County

Utica Reservoir
Stanislaus National Forest, Alpine County

SPREAD OVER FOUR Northern California counties, Stanislaus National Forest borders the northwest edge of Yosemite National Park in the Sierra Nevada. It was established on February 22, 1897, making it one of the country's oldest national forests. There are 811 miles of rivers and streams along with 78 lakes in its 898,099 acres.

Enjoying any of the recreational waters in Stanislaus National Forest comes with a risk, however. The streams are allegedly home to a ghoulish siren that would like nothing more than to drown you and eat your flesh. Many folks have peered into one of the forest's many bodies of water only to see the creature's witch's face staring back at them. The demon has been described as having scaly skin, an evil grin, and sharp, jagged teeth.

The monster never leaves her watery abode, but if you wade into or try to ford a river or stream, she'll grab hold of you and pull you under. Whitewater rafters and kayakers aren't safe either.

The water witch apparently has supernatural powers. According to one old wives' tale, the Stanislaus siren caused a woman to fall off her bicycle alongside one of the forest's streams. The cyclist tumbled into the water and immediately felt the fiend's hands grip her legs. Fortunately, the woman's husband was nearby and managed to drag his wife to safety.

Take extra care if you hike the Arnold Rim Trail: It's where the majority of encounters with the siren take place in Stanislaus National Forest.

In Greek mythology, the Sirens were menacing creatures that lived on the rugged cliffs or shoals of a coastline. They were usually depicted as birds with feathered wings and talons but having the heads and upper torsos of women. Their hypnotic singing would entice sailors to move their boats closer to the shore to hear the enchanting voices better. The vessel would be swept against the rocks and sink, killing the seamen.

The most famous story involving the murderous beings is found in Homer's *Odyssey*. On his epic voyage home from the Trojan War, Odysseus had to sail his ship past the island of the Sirens. He was certain that if he were to hear the sirens' song he would jump off the ship and drown while trying to reach them. He was intent on hearing their intoxicating calls, however, but didn't want to endanger his crew. He commanded them to tie him to the mast but plug their own ears with beeswax. Finally, he ordered his men not to release him no matter how much he begged them to do so, thus preventing his death.

Over time, the word "siren" has become a generic term for an alluring female seductress, especially one that turns out to be treacherous or deadly. But with its pointed teeth and vestiges of scales, the creature inhabiting the Stanislaus National Forest waterways seems to have more in common with the fabled Siren than its human counterpart.

The Stanislaus National Forest may have a water witch in its rivers and creeks, but the Utica Reservoir, also located in the woods south of Lake Tahoe, has a very different kind of spirit haunting it.

The ghost is a little boy who's spotted in the water not too far from shore. Those who think he's real and in trouble should carefully consider before jumping in to rescue him. The phantom will elude anyone who tries to grab hold of it or simply disappear. Then, when the would-be rescuer comes out of the water, his or her body will be covered with huge, painful boils. To quote the old saying: No good deed goes unpunished.

Haunted Trails

Arnold Rim Trail

The mid-elevation Arnold Rim Trail is 7.4 miles out and back. The path is moderately trafficked and of moderate difficulty. There are numerous entrances to Arnold Rim Trail, but there are three main access points. The northernmost is at the Sierra Nevada Logging Museum in White Pines. The first mile of the trail is paved. **Trailhead GPS: N38 15.963' / W120 20.655'**

An entrance off Valley View Drive provides the shortest hike to two popular destinations on the trail: Top of the World and Cougar Route. Be advised that Valley View becomes a dirt road after it leaves the residential area, and it can be potholed, muddy, and slippery. Vehicles with high clearance are strongly advised. **Valley View Trailhead GPS: N38 13.198' / W120 22.674'**

A third entrance to the trail is close to the intersection of Avery Sheep Ranch Road (FR 5N95Y) and Valley View Drive. **Trailhead GPS: N 38 13.373' / W120 22.700'**

Arnold Rim Trail is popular with hikers, mountain bikers, and equestrians, and sections have various degrees of difficulty. The vistas include canyons, a waterfall, several streams, dense woods, and high, rocky outcrops. For a full backpacking experience, Arnold Rim Trail can be linked to other paths for a 35-mile hike from the East Bay area all the way to the eastern slope of the Sierras. A map of the entire trail can be found at https://arnoldrimtrail.org/trail-information/arnold-rim-trail-map.

Hikers report that there can be a high number of mosquitoes on the trail. Maybe the Stanislaus siren won't be your greatest nemesis.

Utica Reservoir

Unless otherwise posted, camping is allowed anywhere along Utica Reservoir's boulder- and tree-lined shore, as well as on some of its islands. No motorized crafts are allowed on the reservoir, but paddling and kayaking are permitted, as is fishing.

11

Natural Wonders

Chilnualna Falls Trail, Bridalveil Fall Trail, Tenaya Canyon
Yosemite National Park, Mariposa County

Dry Creek Running Trail
Modesto, Stanislaus County

WITH ITS THUNDERING waterfalls, towering granite cliffs, crystal-clear streams, lakes, and meadowlands, Yosemite National Park is a piece of heaven on earth. Its signature sights include Half Dome, El Capitan, Glacier Point, Yosemite Falls, and Bridalveil Fall, and three separate groves of sequoia. Attracting more than 4 million visitors annually, it is one of the most popular national parks in America.

But for hikers and campers, Yosemite also has a dark side, and many backpackers have had ghostly encounters—some of them deadly.

Glaciers carved out Yosemite Valley eons ago, and by the time of the California gold rush in the mid-1800s, Yosemite Valley had been occupied for 8,000–10,000 years. The Native Americans living there called the valley Ahwahnee (meaning "big mouth").

As more and more miners, traders, and pioneers arrived from the East, competition between the settlers and the native tribes for land and resources grew fierce—not just in Yosemite, but all over California. In

Bridalveil Fall, Yosemite National Park.
PHOTO COURTESY OF TOM OGDEN

1851, as part of a regional campaign to end Native American resistance, US Army major Jim Savage led the Mariposa Battalion into Yosemite Valley. They were pursuing 200 Ahwahnechee led by Chief Tenaya. The chief's forces were defeated, their village was destroyed, and they were relocated to a reservation near Fresno.

Sadly, the story of Chief Tenaya did not end well. After a few months in captivity, he and a few of his men were allowed to return to Yosemite Valley, but in the spring of 1852 they attacked eight gold miners. The Ahwahnechee fled to the neighboring Mono tribe, who gave them shelter—that is, until the newcomers stole some of their hosts' horses and took off. The Mono tracked their ungrateful guests and killed most of them, including Chief Tenaya. Eventually the US government allowed Native Americans to return to the valley.

Dr. Lafayette Bunnell, who accompanied Savage's army unit, later wrote a book, *The Discovery of Yosemite*, about the breathtaking vistas he encountered. In fact, he's credited with giving the valley its English name, Yosemite. The word was derived from the language of the Miwok, who also lived in the surrounding area. The tribe called the valley Yohhe'meti or Yosse'meti (meaning "killer" or "those who kill"), an unflattering allusion to the Ahwahnechee, with whom they frequently fought. Besides Bunnell's book, the letters that soldiers sent home also stirred the imagination of people back East. Yosemite Valley was no longer a secret.

There were endless marvels for arriving tourists to experience. In 1857 Galen Clark, an early settler, discovered a cluster of giant sequoia, now called the Mariposa Grove, just outside Yosemite Valley in the village of Wawona. The Wawona Hotel, still operating today, was opened in 1879 to accommodate visitors. Two small groups of sequoia, the Tuolumne and Merced Groves, were discovered later and were subsequently added to Yosemite National Park.

Early on, Clark and others recognized that without intervention from the federal government, commercial interests such as grazing, logging, and mining would soon threaten the natural wonders of Yosemite Valley. Eventually Congress took up their petitions. In 1864 President Abraham Lincoln signed the Yosemite Grant to protect the valley, but the land was to be administered by California as a state park. Galen Clark was named Yosemite's first civil guardian three years later.

Yosemite finally became a national park in 1890, with Clark as its first ranger. Two of the park's main features, however, Yosemite Valley and Mariposa Grove, remained under California state control. In 1903 famed naturalist and preservationist John Muir led President Theodore Roosevelt on a three-day camping trip through Yosemite, during which he convinced the chief executive to extend federal protection to Yosemite Valley and Mariposa Grove. After the US National Park System was created in 1916, the federal government took over all jurisdictions from the state. Today, the park encompasses 1,169 square miles in the western

Sierra Nevada. Almost 95 percent of the land is designated as wilderness. Yosemite National Park straddles four California counties: Mono, Madera, Tuolumne, and Mariposa. In 1984 it was named a World Heritage Site.

The first tourist concessions on the valley floor were opened in 1884. In 1899 David and Jennie Curry were granted permission to build a few cabins and campsites, which they collectively called Curry Village. Later the site's name was changed to the more rustic Camp Curry. Today the campground is known as Half Dome Village, and it's the largest lodging area in Yosemite.

The most luxurious place to stay in Yosemite Valley National Park is the Ahwahnee Hotel, which was founded in 1927. (From 2016 to 2019, it was known as the Majestic Yosemite Hotel.) It boasts ninety-seven rooms and twenty-four adjacent cottages, all situated near the base of Half Dome. The main building's primary ghost is Mary Curry Tresidder, a former manager, who died there in 1970. Her apparition has been seen by guests and staff alike as it drifts down the halls, seemingly making her nightly rounds. She manifests most often on the sixth floor, which Tresidder had converted into her private living quarters.

Many of the Ahwahnee ghost legends date back to World War II. During the conflict, the US Navy turned the hotel into a temporary convalescent hospital, which might explain some of the paranormal activity that's been encountered on the mezzanine and the third floor.

There's also an old wives' tale about a young woman who worked at the Ahwahnee Hotel during this period. She was having a clandestine affair with a pilot, even though he was already married. Any hope of a happy resolution evaporated when he was killed in combat. Now the ghost of the unknown woman wanders the vast meadow located behind the hotel.

Also of interest to ghost enthusiasts, several of the public spaces inside the Ahwahnee Hotel inspired set designs for the 1980 film *The Shining*. (Author Stephen King based the story, however, on the haunted Stanley Hotel in Estes Park, Colorado, where he once stayed as a guest.)

Elsewhere in Yosemite National Park, a spectral couple has been spotted at Stoneman Bridge, close to where they drowned. The phantom of a man who hanged himself now roams the campsites. He's also occasionally been seen swinging from the wooden frame inside one of the tents. According to several of the park staff, invisible hands sometimes move spoons or slam doors in the employee residence dorms. There have also been scattered reports of people seeing spectres in the forests, especially those of Native Americans in nineteen-century garb. Then there's the curse that Chief Tenaya laid on (what is now called) Tenaya Canyon, the route he used when he was forced out of Yosemite Valley in 1851. He swore that anyone who entered the canyon would have a fatal fall, get swept away in a flash flood, or die of exposure. Or they might simply disappear.

The National Park Service estimates there are about 800 miles of unpaved trails in Yosemite. There are another 20 miles of surfaced walking paths and 214 miles of paved roads open to motor vehicles.

One of the macadam footpaths leads to the bottom of 620-foot Bridalveil Fall. According to an ancient legend of the Miwok, a malevolent spirit named Po-ho-no (literally meaning "evil wind") inhabits the waterfall and haunts its crest. In one version of the tale, an old Native American woman was beckoned to the top of the waterfall by Po-ho-no, only to have the spirit "push" (i.e., blow) her over. The woman's body was never found, and her spirit joined Po-ho-no to help entice others to their death. A variation says that the victim was, instead, a young Ahwahnechee maiden who was out gathering grass for weaving. After her tragic plunge, her remains, too, were never found. In this telling, Po-ho-no held her spirit captive until she enticed another person to the falls. Only then was the maiden released to join her ancestors. And so it would continue, with the spirit of each new victim luring the next to certain doom.

Even today the unseen entity will supposedly draw an unsuspecting person to the top of the cascade, resulting in his or her death. It's said sometimes that even those who have no intention of going anywhere near the waterfall will hear Po-ho-no whispering in their ears, and they feel compelled to try to climb to the top. For safety's sake, there's no path to the crest of the falls.

Although Po-ho-no is most often associated with Bridalveil Fall, the spirit has been blamed for fatal plunges at almost every cascade in Yosemite at one time or another. A recent reemergence of the myth came in 2011 when three hikers were swept over Vernal Falls at the opposite end of the valley.

Of course, backpackers can lose their balance on slippery rocks. Even an expert swimmer can be swept away by a strong current, especially when Yosemite's rivers and streams are gorged in the spring. But could all of the waterfall deaths have been accidents? Or carelessness? Or were some of them caused by the lethal spirit gust, Po-ho-no?

The general public wasn't aware of one of Yosemite's most durable ghost stories until Galen Clark published his tale about the "Crying Boy" in a 1904 magazine. He recounted how in September 1857 he had taken a "long tramp" to Grouse Lake, a small body of water located about 8 miles high above Wawona. Clark claimed that while resting on the shore, he heard a "distinct wailing cry, somewhat like a puppy when lost." Later that night, he happened to meet several Ahwahnechee, and he told them about the odd sound he had heard.

The rest of Clark's account is best told in his own words:

They replied that it was not a dog—that a long time ago an Indian boy had been drowned in the lake, and that every time anyone passed there he always cried after them, and no one dared go into the lake, for [the boy's ghost] would catch them by the legs and pull them down and they would be drowned. I then concluded that it must have been some unseen waterfowl that made that cry, and at that time I thought that the Indians were trying to impose on my credulity, but I am now convinced they fully believed the story they told me.

The legend of Grouse Lake persists. Trekkers still sometimes hear the spectre's anguished calls for help and are tempted to try to save the boy, even though they can't spot him. And if they do jump into the water, well, you know the rest. Most hikers to the remote alpine lake access it via the Chilnualna Falls Trail, an 8.4-mile loop that has three waterfalls. As a bonus for ghost hunters, it's claimed that Po-ho-no haunts the uppermost cascade.

You might have an otherworldly visitor even if you stay overnight in a hotel just outside the valley. Galen Clark's Wawona Hotel, now the Big Trees Lodge, is haunted by the phantom of a pilot whose plane crashed on the grounds during the 1920s. Too injured to be transported to a hospital, he was carried to Moore Cottage, which had been added to the property in 1894. Unfortunately the man died, and almost immediately his spirit began to appear in and around the bungalow, wearing his leather jacket, cap and goggles, and white silk scarf.

Yosemite View Lodge is located along the Merced River in El Portal on CA 140, the northern entrance to the park. For years, guests have been waking up to see a ghost in their rooms. Usually it's a dark shadowy figure, but one woman, a writer, reported that the spectre is a little girl. In fact, she caught sight of the silent apparition four times during her short stay at the inn.

If you're entering or leaving Yosemite National Park through its western gateway, you may want to stop to hike Dry Creek Running Trail in Modesto. The path is haunted by the ghost of a teenage boy who committed suicide by jumping off a bridge on Claus Road.

According to the legend, the lad was a poor farmworker. He rescued the daughter of the town banker out on the trail after her horse and carriage ran off, and soon the two were in love. Knowing that her father would disapprove of the young man, the girl began to meet the farmhand in secret. Unfortunately, their rendezvous were discovered. The father forbade his daughter from ever seeing the boy again. Two months later, the father married off the girl to a wealthy businessman in another town. The young man, distraught, took his own life.

Though recognizable as a teenage boy, the spectre is not much more than a shadow. He's been seen all along Dry Creek Running Trail, but he most often appears where it intersects Claus Road. The phantom remains motionless after being spotted, and he vanishes as soon as he's approached.

Haunted Trails

Bridalveil Fall

Most people access Yosemite's Bridalveil Fall from a large parking area located on the right side of Wawona Road, close to where the street merges into Southside Drive. It's a simple 0.5-mile walk to the falls from the far side of the lot. **Trailhead GPS: N37 42.995' / W119 39.071'**

Others prefer to travel a few hundred yards on Southside Drive, park on the side of the road, and hike a slightly longer trail (an additional 0.25 mile) offering different views of the falls before it meets up with the more direct path. Both walkways are paved. The trail—and you—will be soaked by heavy spray as you near the cascade. The waterfall was named for its ever-present mist, which to some fancifully resembles a bride's veil. Because of the ease of the "trail" and the fact that virtually every tour bus stops there, it's one of the most crowded walks in Yosemite.

There are no established trails that lead to the top of Bridalveil Fall. Don't even think about trying to reach it!

Grouse Lake

Other than its paranormal connection, Grouse Lake is not a major attraction in and of itself. It's a minor alpine lake at an altitude of about 8,300 feet. Those who do visit it usually arrive via a 0.1-mile connector path from the Chilnualna Falls Trail. There's a parking lot that can accommodate about a dozen cars at the trailhead on Chilnualna Road in the village of Wawoma. **Trailhead GPS: N37 32.903' / W119 38.040'**

The hike just to the falls is a strenuous 4.6 miles with a 2,300-foot elevation gain. Continue on Chilnualna Falls Trail past the cascades. There will be a connecting trail to Grouse Lake off to the right in about 4.2 miles. There are usually no signposts for the turnoff, but the path appears on most hiking maps. If you reach the better-marked Crescent Lake, you've gone too far. This excursion might make a better overnight backpacking trip than a one-day out-and-back hike.

Tenaya Canyon

For those wanting to make a descent through Tenaya Canyon, the trailhead is located on Tioga Road at the western end of Tenaya Lake, about 16 miles from Yosemite's Tioga Pass entrance. Look for the "Sunrise" or "Sunrise/Clouds Rest" signs. There's enough parking for about a dozen cars at the trailhead. **Trailhead GPS: N37 49.551' / W119 28.228'**

For those who want to have a taste of the cursed canyon but lack mountaineering ability, a 3.5-mile round-trip route covers the upper canyon. About 0.5 mile from the trailhead, you'll reach Tenaya Creek. Leave the marked Sunrise/Clouds Rest Trail and follow the creek downstream. (By the end of summer, it may be a dry, though recognizable, creek bed rather than a stream.) You will pass through talus fields, and at some places will have to hop a bit from boulder to boulder. At about 1.5 miles from the trailhead, you'll see a National Park Service marker cautioning underequipped or inexperienced hikers to turn back and return to Tioga Road. Know your limits, and heed the warning accordingly.

The full 4,200-foot descent through Tenaya Canyon is extremely demanding, holding a Grade III Alpine Climbing NCSS Rating and an ACA technical canyoning rating of 3B IV, three stars. The one-way 10-mile route down to Mirror Creek requires proficiency in multiple advanced skills, including route navigation, creek and pool fording, the use of climbing gear, and rappelling.

The complete descent should only be attempted by experienced canyoneers. Even if you encounter no major hang-ups, the hike, top to bottom, takes 10 to 11 hours. The descent is best in late summer and early fall when the water level in Tenaya Creek (which runs through the canyon) is at its lowest. Those wishing to tackle the entire descent should do further research to carefully plan and equip their hike before setting out.

Haunted Accommodations near Yosemite

Big Trees Lodge
8308 Wawoma Rd.
Yosemite Valley, CA 95389
(888) 413-8869

Yosemite View Lodge
11136 CA 140
El Portal, CA 95318
(209) 379-2681

Dry Creek Trail
Dry Creek Trail in Modesto is an easy, moderately trafficked 8.8-mile out-and-back hike. The route could be considered a loop because there are alternate paths for the return. The trailhead is on Claus Road. **Trailhead GPS: N37 39.20.016' / W120 55.14.124'**

12

The Lake Spirits

Coldwater Campground, Lake George Campground, Lake Mary Campground, Mammoth Mountain RV Park, McGee Creek RV Park and Campground, New Shady Rest Campground, Old Shady Rest Campground, Pine Glen Group Campground, Sherwin Creek Campground, Twin Lakes
Mammoth Lakes, Mono County

Doris Lake, Florence Lake, Mono, Old Pedro, Evolution Valley, Range of Light, Mono Hot Springs Campgrounds, Old Pedro, Hot Springs Resort, San Joaquin River
Mono Hot Springs, Fresno County

MAMMOTH LAKES IS one of the most popular recreation areas in California. Skiers are drawn to Mammoth Mountain from late fall to early spring, and its many lakes and endless hiking paths draw the summer crowd. Stories about ghosts and other nocturnal creatures have frightened overnight guests in the campgrounds at Mammoth Lakes for decades.

A Fresno couple staying at Coldwater Campground was eating at one of the picnic tables when they saw a black bear coming swiftly toward them. Glued to the spot in fear, they were stunned when a young woman with long black hair came out of nowhere and stepped directly in front of the beast. The animal took one look at the woman, turned, and loped away. The pair's grateful joy instantly turned to terror when the mysterious Good Samaritan spun in their direction. Her face was rotted away, with only hollow sockets for eyes. Though the ghoul was hideous, it's unknown whether she was good or evil. The couple didn't stay around long enough to find out.

The experience that another couple had at Lake George Campground has all the elements of a classic ghost story. They went skinny-dipping in the lake that night, even though they knew swimming was prohibited—with or without clothing. The young woman saw her boyfriend duck below the surface, and almost instantly she felt a pair of hands grasp her legs. She immediately realized the hands were too small to be her boyfriend's—plus they were trying to drag her under. Then the man popped up some distance away only to see his girlfriend struggling to keep her head above water. He rushed to help her, but a second set of hands pushed him away.

After an intense struggle, the young man finally managed to get free, reach his girlfriend, and pull her ashore. They had no explanation for what they encountered—that is, until they developed the photographs from their vacation. In every photo that showed them together, there were two ghostly boys with bluish skin standing directly behind them, even though no one had been there when the picture was taken. The couple later found out that twin brothers had drowned in the lake years earlier.

Lake Mary Campground has a deserved reputation for being one of the best-located campsites around Mammoth Lakes. It also seems to be the home of several spectral children with deep-set black eyes, who are usually seen among the pine trees at the edges of the campground. A female camper happened to bump into one of them during a night stroll in the forest. Thinking the little girl was lost, she asked her name—Ella—took her hand, and led her back toward camp. As they came into the light, the woman saw that the child was actually a ghost!

The woman dropped Ella's hand, ran into her tent, and zipped up the flaps. The spectre stood outside and loudly began to cry. She claimed she was hurt and begged to come inside the tent. As hard as it was to resist

Ella's plea, the camper refused. Come dawn, the ghostly girl was gone. The woman later discovered that no one else in the campground had seen or heard the little girl the previous night.

A dangerous spirit is said to call out to people who are inside campers and tents at Mammoth Mountain RV Park. If anyone is foolish enough to open a door or tent flap, the creature grabs hold of the person and pulls him or her outside. Often, this is the last time the victim is seen.

The spectre of an elderly man is spotted hobbling around McGee Creek RV Park and Campground. Those who go up to him are unaccountably overwhelmed by a sense of fear or danger. No one knows who the ghost was, why he haunts the campsite, or why he instills such anxiety in those who try to interact with him.

New Shady Rest Campground is surrounded by Jeffrey pines and offers RV parking as well as campsites for tents. According to an old wives' tale, campers occasionally fall prey to a chimerical creature known as a *lechuza* that lives in the neighboring woods. In Mexican and Tejano folklore, a *lechuza* is a woman who has sold her soul to the devil in exchange for magical powers to become a bruja (that is, a sorceress or witch).

Lechuza are shape-shifters. By day, they look human; at night they keep their human heads but have owl-like bodies with talons strong enough to lift an adult. (In this form, they look similar to the Sirens of Greek and Roman myth.

Legend has it that the *lechuza* at New Shady Rest Campground was fleeing through the nearby woods in human form when she was attacked and killed by a black bear. Now bound to that area of the forest for all eternity, she'll occasionally swoop down on unsuspecting New Shady Rest campers and carry them away.

Old Shady Rest Campground is located on the west side of Sawmill Cutoff, just across the road from New Shady Rest, and it has a spectral nighttime visitor of its own. While alive, the ghost was an outlaw, infamous for robbing stagecoaches and killing all of the passengers. The law finally found him hiding out near the present-day campgrounds and shot him. Some versions of the legend say that his body was deliberately left there, out in the open, so mountain lions and bears could devour it. Regardless, the murderous bandit has returned in spirit form and is just as homicidal as ever.

In one oft-told tale, a couple awoke in the middle of the night to hear scratching on the outside of their trailer. The husband went to investigate, but when he didn't return after a few minutes, the woman went out to find him. What she saw was horrifying: Her husband was struggling with a dark, smokelike spectre, which was trying to smother him. The wife screamed, waking up everyone in the surrounding campers. When they turned on their outside lights to see what was going on, the sudden illumination spooked the ghost, and it promptly vanished.

An invisible spirit in the Pine Glen Group Campground attacked four male students from Fresno City College. The young men had deliberately set up camp some distance from other people, so they were intrigued when they heard the sound of laughter outside their tents. Two of the guys went out to look around. They were immediately knocked over and savagely pummeled by invisible fists. Then the students who had stayed inside their tent were dragged out by an unseen entity and bashed with their own camping gear. The assault went on for half an hour. Then everything abruptly stopped. They heard a disembodied laugh, a voice call "good-bye," and the ordeal was over.

The phantom of a young girl shows up at Sherwin Creek Campground, dressed all in white. She's said to be the spirit of a 14-year-old who was sacrificed by Satanists nearby. Even before she materializes, people hear her shrieks as she begs for her life. When she does appear, her face is branded with inverted crosses, and blood flows from slashes on her body. Although she'll rush at people without warning, so far she's always disappeared before she caught anyone.

Over at the Twin Lakes, the ghosts of people who drowned there will drag you under to suffer the same fate. The vengeful dead have also been blamed for people never surfacing after falling out of their boats.

The phantoms will even come out to capture you if get too close to the water's edge. One hiker claimed he was walking a trail by the lakes in 2010 when he saw an eerie, dark circle appear on the water's surface. It grew larger and larger, and then, suddenly, a pair of hands burst out of the water. He thought he was far enough away to be safe, but then he felt a clammy hand wrap around the back of his neck. He passed out. When he came to, he was facedown on the ground, only inches from the lake. He was one of the lucky ones. For some reason, the spirits let him go.

Few things are more relaxing than a long soak in a hot pool fed by natural springs—that is, unless you wind up sharing it with a ghost.

Mono Hot Springs is located about 25 miles south of Mammoth Lakes on the western slope of the Sierra Nevada between Yosemite and Kings Canyon National Parks. Before the arrival of settlers from the East, the Mono tribe of Native Americans inhabited the area. In fact, it was these indigenous people who first showed the springs to the pioneers and explained the health benefits of bathing in the mineral waters.

Until the end of the nineteenth century, the springs could only be accessed by horseback or foot. Even then it was a 60-mile trip from Auberry, the closest small town, and the trek would take at least four days.

In 1910 Southern California Edison began construction on a system of tunnels, hydroelectric generators, and power stations linking the lakes around Mono Hot Springs to provide electricity for Los Angeles. An expansion in 1920 led to a paved road being built over Kaiser Pass, and the last 6 miles from Huntington Lake to Mono Hot Springs was finally opened to the public in 1927.

Once Mono Hot Springs was accessible by car, visits rapidly increased. In 1934 the Depression-era Civilian Conservation Corps erected a bathhouse, campgrounds, and ancillary buildings at the springs along the San Joaquin River. Many of early guests were Japanese visitors and immigrants, because the pools reminded them of the mineral hot springs back home.

In 1935 the USDA Forest Service issued a permit to Walter Hill to build a resort at Mono Hot Springs. Its first few cabins and a general store opened in 1937, and by 1949 there were twenty-four cabins and a cafe in addition to the market. Frank Winslow bought the resort in 1963, and his family still operates it to this day.

Of course, you don't have to stay at the resort to enjoy the hot springs in the area, many of which are not part of the resort. For overnighters, the forest service maintains the Mono Hot Springs Campground, nestled among aspen and pine at an elevation of 6,700 feet. There are picnic tables, vault toilets, and bear-proof storage lockers, but drinking water is not available. Please note that while camping trailers are allowed, large RVs are not recommended on Kaiser Pass Road. Reservations for a campsite must be made at least three days in advance (877-444-6777 or recreation .gov).

A popular hiking destination from the Mono Hot Springs Resort is Doris Lake, which is fed by underground springs. The water temperature is generally about 70 degrees, so swimming is best from mid-June through Labor Day. The large body of water has about a half dozen large rock formations along its shore.

Once you get to Doris Lake, you may not be alone. It's not just fellow hikers who frequent the trails around the shoreline. They're also haunted by an unidentified "Woman in White," so called because of the color she always wears.

One of the many stories about her tells of a husband, wife, and their teenage sons who hiked to Doris Lake for an early evening swim. Just as they were about to jump into the water, they all spotted the apparition. The ghost was still at quite a distance away but clearly visible. The spectre called out to the sons, asking them whether they had seen her boyfriend, James. She repeated the question over and over as she drew closer to the puzzled onlookers.

It was then that the mother got a good look at the phantom's face. It was rotted away, as if the stranger had been dead for years. The folks fled, but the father later reported that everyone in the family had chills and fever for the next three days.

The Woman in White at Doris Lake is the most commonly reported wraith at Mono Hot Springs, but there are numerous others you might run into. One haunts Florence Lake. A couple was kayaking when the female's boat flipped over without warning. When the woman, who was an experienced swimmer, didn't immediately surface, the man dove in to rescue her. He was shocked to see a green hag with long hair and a ghastly, decaying face clutching his partner from behind, one hand around her waist and the other covering her mouth. The man immediately began to wrestle with the infernal creature. The monster eventually released her captive and vanished into the depths of the lake.

An unknown entity at Mono Hot Springs Resort has startled visitors staying in the old stone cabins. Occasionally a guest will begin to feel a general sense of unease around midnight. Then a vaporous human figure floats through the locked door. It crosses the room, stands at the foot of the bed for a few moments, and then evaporates. If the lodger dares to touch the ethereal interloper, his or her hand is burned as if the ghost were scalding hot.

There are several spirits lurking inside the River Rock Cafe at the resort. One is thought to be a little child, due to its distinctive, disembodied laugh. People have felt the cold, damp hands of an invisible spirit touch the back of their necks and seen a steely set of eyes—just eyes—glare out from one the restaurant's mirrors. There have also been reports of floating silverware!

A hiker shared the tale of his spooky visit to the resort's post office. He went up to the counter, but the postman, dressed in early twentieth-century garb, ignored the young man completely. The customer then noticed a woman at the far end of the room and went over to complain about her coworker's conduct. The woman was baffled and said that she was the only one on duty that day. When they looked to where the "mailman" had been standing, no one was there.

Another time, two campers were awakened around 4 a.m. by the sound of horse hooves outside their tent. They opened the flap and saw a large stagecoach and a team of horses standing there, but no driver or passengers. Next they heard the crack of a whip, and the horses and coach rambled away. When the pair rewoke later that morning, they curiously checked around the tent. There was no sign that a stagecoach or horses had ever been there.

According to another popular legend, three women were relaxing in the Old Pedro hot spring when they heard something splashing in the nearby San Joaquin River. A man dressed as a cowboy suddenly appeared and started walking toward them. They greeted him, but the man said nothing. When he kept coming in their direction, silent and unresponsive, the women became frightened and huddled together in one corner of the pool. To their amazement, the stranger stepped onto the surface of the water and, instead of sinking, walked straight across the pool. He continued into the brush, out of sight, and never returned.

The phantom cowboy may not be the only ghost that haunts that section of the San Joaquin River. An angler was standing on the banks one morning when he noticed a sudden unseasonably cold wind coming from the forest behind him. Almost immediately he was overcome with feelings of melancholy and dread. The psychic attack didn't stop until another fisherman showed up, and the unseen "presence" dissipated.

Scared yet? If you are, don't even think about hiking or camping in the section of the High Sierra known as the Range of Light. This wilderness area between Yosemite and Kings Canyon is purportedly inhabited by a mischievous race of "little people," similar to pixies or elves. The puckish creatures may come up behind you and shake your backpack, trip you, or blow dust and sand into your eyes. The playful imps are seldom if ever seen, but many people have reported spotting their tiny footprints.

Just a few miles to the southeast of Mono Hot Springs, an otherworldly being has been known to disturb campers in Evolution Valley. One woman tells of her overnight encounter with a ghost in the High Sierra. She arrived by horseback, traveling alone, and set up her tent as usual. Partway into the night she was awakened by a crushing weight on top of her sleeping bag. She opened her eyes to see another pair of eyes, glowing red, staring down at her. She screamed, and the creature, apparently startled, left the tent. But whatever it was, it didn't go away. Throughout the night, every time the terrified woman tried to get to her horse, the beast dragged her back and forced her into the tent. It wasn't until daybreak that the strange intruder was gone, and the woman was able to escape.

But odds are low that any of this stuff will happen to you, right?

Haunted Trails

The trail from Mono Hot Springs Resort to Doris Lake is an out-and-back 1.1-mile hike. It has moderate traffic and an elevation gain of only 249 feet. The pathway is at its prettiest in May, when wildflowers are in bloom. It's comfortable hiking until the first snows around October. Dogs are allowed on the trail, but they must be kept on a leash. Maps are available at the resort's general store, ranger stations, and online. A real-time GPS on your mobile phone is recommended, because hikers have reported missing signage at the multiple forks in the trail. **Trailhead GPS: N37 19.880' / W119 01.199'**

13

The Phantom of Moro Rock

High Sierra Trail, Giant Forest Loop Trail, Moro Rock,
Crystal Cave
Sequoia National Park, Tulare County

T**HERE'S NO QUESTION** that most people visit Sequoia National
Park to wander among its monumental trees. Tall and gigantic
in circumference, the sequoias are closely related to their redwood cousins on the coast. For fans of the paranormal, however,
the park's major draws are two haunted landmarks: Moro Rock
and Crystal Cave.

Long before the arrival of European settlers, the region that today
makes up Sequoia National Park was inhabited primarily by the Monache
(or Western Mono) Native Americans, but by the time pioneers moved
west of the Sierras, there were few left. One of the first nonnative settlers
was Hale Tharp, a rancher, who is remembered for the unusual cabin he
built by hollowing out a fallen sequoia. Tharp's Log, as it's now known, has
never been moved and can be visited.

Although there was an attempt to set up logging operations in the
area in the 1880s, only a few thousand trees were leveled. Fortunately, it
was discovered early on that the trees' wood easily splintered, making the
timber unsuitable for construction.

Sequoia National Park was formed in 1890 to protect about 404,000
acres of forested mountainside. There are many groves of sequoia in the

park, but perhaps the most accessible is the Giant Forest, which encompasses 1,880 acres. Five of the ten most massive trees on earth can be found within the Giant Forest, including the biggest of them all, the General Sherman Tree.

Also located within Sequoia National Park at its eastern edge is Mount Whitney, which, at 14,505 feet, is the tallest mountain in the contiguous United States. Directly to the north and abutting Sequoia National Park is Kings Canyon National Park. In fact, the National Park Service administers them together as Sequoia and Kings Canyon National Parks. Eighty-four percent of the two parks' land is designated as wilderness.

Moro Rock is located between Giant Forest and Crescent Meadow, and it comes with an eerie story. Supposedly around midnight, a headless apparition materializes on top of the 6,725-foot granite dome. If you approach the spirit, he tries to grab you before he screams and leaps off the rock "to his death." Fortunately, so far his attempts to take anyone with him have been unsuccessful.

Don't let this old wives' tale deter you from taking the hike to the top. The 360-degree view from the peak is spectacular. It's possible to see most of the park and as far as the Great Western Divide. The ascent is made via 400 stairs chiseled and cemented into place by the Civilian Conservation Corps in 1931. The well-maintained path, handrailed in some places for safety, is listed on the National Register of Historic Places. The climb to the summit is both figuratively and literally breathtaking—whether or not you see the ghost.

Finally, there are more than 250 caves in Sequoia National Park, but only one of them, Crystal Cave, is open commercially. The cavern, discovered in 1918, is located very close to the Giant Forest. It's thought that the CCC workers occasionally camped inside the entrance to Crystal Cave in the 1940s for protection from the weather, and it's believed Native Americans stayed there long before that. Local lore says some of the spirits from both groups have returned to inhabit the cavern.

Perhaps the park's motto should be "Come for the sequoias, stay for the spooks."

Haunted Trails

High Sierra Trail

For truly adventuresome visitors to Sequoia National Park, the 59-mile, heavily trafficked High Sierra Trail, often abbreviated HST, will take you up and over the Great Divide. Needless to say, the hike is considered difficult and takes several days. There are many established campsites along the way. The western trailhead is in Crescent Meadow in Sequoia National Park. **Trailhead GPS: N36 33.281' / W118 44.927'**. The trail ends at Whitney Portal. **Whitney Portal GPS: N36 52.224' / W118 14.399'**

Giant Forest Loop Trail

There are numerous trails within Giant Forest, but the most popular is probably the easy, paved, 7-mile Giant Forest Loop Trail. The first part of the hike (which is the busiest) is called Sherman Tree Trail. This 0.8-mile round-trip section takes visitors as far as its namesake tree. The remainder of the loop, called Congress Trail, winds through dozens of the immense trees and is less trafficked. **Loop Trailhead GPS: N36 35.099' / W118 44.972'**

14

Death Valley Days

Barker Ranch, Wingate Pass, Hells Gate, Racetrack Playa, Skidoo,
Amargosa Opera House and Hotel
Death Valley National Park, Inyo County

ITS VERY NAME conjures up images of vast desolation. Death Valley National Park is the hottest, most arid, and lowest point in all of North America. It encompasses 3 million acres and is about the size of the state of Connecticut. The only US national parks that are larger are the four located in Alaska. The desert itself was recognized as a national monument in 1933. Over the years, more and more protected land was added until, in 1994, the expanded site was declared a national park.

Death Valley is filled with places bearing forbidding names such as Dante's View, Coffin Peak, Devil's Cornfield, and the Funeral Mountains. Nevertheless, it's a place of stark beauty and surprises. In the spring, for instance, the floor of parts of the valley can be covered with wildflowers.

Most people think that Death Valley received its ominous name from the dozens or even hundreds of people meeting their end in the isolated location, dying of thirst, exposure, or hunger after going off-trail and becoming lost. In fact, it got its name after a member of a group of prospectors—just one—died on their way to the gold rush after being stranded in the winter of 1849–50.

Although there was short-lived gold mining in Death Valley during the late nineteenth and early twentieth centuries, the only mineral to be mined on a regular basis was borax, and as an old advertising slogan mentioned, it was brought out on wagons pulled by twenty-mule teams.

Backpacking in Death Valley can be both exhausting and exhilarating. Part of the excitement is the chance of coming face to face with some of its many ghosts.

For example, hike up Warm Springs Canyon Road to reach Barker Ranch, a hideout of the Charles Manson Family from 1968 to 1969. In addition to masterminding the 1969 Sharon Tate murders in Benedict Canyon in Los Angeles, Manson (or his followers) are thought to have also killed several people at the ranch, even though no bodies have ever been found there.

A fire swept through the abandoned house in 2009, leaving only the stone walls intact. Still, the ranch remains a popular campsite, especially for those who enjoy tales of murder and the macabre. Visitors have had the disturbing feeling they were being watched. They've also heard astral screams or disembodied chanting, and some folks detected the noxious odor of rotting flesh. There's also the apparition of an unidentified man in a white robe that wanders the immediate area. The fire-gutted house has been fenced off, so it's no longer possible to go inside. But many people in the past reported having nightmares while staying inside the cabin overnight; some of their dreams were of Manson trying to persuade them to join his cult.

For centuries, the Cahroc native inhabitants had passed down tales of a civilization of light-skinned people with a strange language that lived in an underground city at Wingate Pass. Early Europeans claimed to have discovered a series of caves in the region that emitted strange green lights.

Charles Manson believed that Devils Hole, a water-filled cave in the pass, was one of the entrances to the mythic subterranean city described by the Cahroc. He planned to one day swim through the "portal" to the other side but was captured before he had the chance to try. At least two people have drowned in the attempt. Devils Hole is in Nevada, just over the state line from Death Valley Junction.

In 1931 amateur explorer Dr. F. Bruce Russell announced he had found a cavern near Wingate Pass containing several 8-foot-tall mummies and unusual, unrecognizable relics. He claimed that over the next fifteen years he discovered and investigated thirty-two similar caves, all within a 7-mile radius. Russell attempted to secure financing to retrieve the artifacts in 1947, but investors demanded to see some proof the items existed. With no one to corroborate his claims, Russell went back to Death Valley to retrieve some of the objects himself. He never returned.

Perhaps all of this could be explained if another ancient tale is true: Supposedly, flying saucers regularly land in Death Valley, and some UFO enthusiasts suggest that there's an alien base inside one of its many caverns.

Despite its name, Hells Gate is a pleasant area for hiking, horseback riding, and ghost hunting. A house used to stand near the signal tower located there, but fire destroyed it in the 1980s, killing two children and their nanny. All three haunt the site. Hikers have seen the woman's apparition, and she has appeared in photographs. The children don't show themselves, but they make their presence known in a way that's just as creepy. Trekkers sometimes notice a child's toy on the trail as they walk along, but in a few minutes, the same toy will inexplicably be back on the path in front of them. They pass it again. The toy comes back. This is repeated over and over. Each time the toy reappears a bit farther down the trail. In addition to these hauntings, Hells Gate is known for having sudden "cold spots," a phenomenon that's thought to indicate the presence of a spirit.

There's an old cowboy legend throughout the Southwest about a mysterious desert feline that looks like an ordinary house cat except that it's about 2 feet tall. It's called a cactus cat because the critter uses its razor-like claws to slice the plants open to drink the sap. Because the juice can become fermented, there are many comic stories about drunken cactus cats staggering across the wasteland. The creature is a cryptid, not a ghost. None has been seen in Death Valley for decades, but that doesn't necessarily mean they're not there—and real.

Park rangers and repeat visitors to Racetrack Playa in Death Valley National Park may notice something odd. The playa is a chalky, dry, flat former lakebed, but it's strewn with large rocks that move on their own—sometimes as far as 1,500 feet! No one has ever seen them rolling, but the boulders, some of them weighing up to 650 pounds, leave noticeable tracks when they reposition themselves. Scientists have offered many theories as to how the rocks shift, from magnetic or gravitational forces to floods or high winds. For now, the phenomenon remains an enigma.

And then there's Skidoo. Once an active gold mining center, all that remains of the place is a mill, several spent mines, a cemetery—and a ghost! The spectre is a former saloon owner, Joe "Hootch" Simpson, who tried to rob the town bank in 1908 and, in the process, gunned down the manager. (Another version of the tale says that Simpson shot him over a $20 debt.) Simpson was captured by an angry mob, lynched, and then buried in the town cemetery. But here's the fun part: When a reporter showed up from Los Angeles a few weeks later, Hootch was unceremoniously dug up and rehanged to stage photographs for the newspaper.

Before Simpson was reinterred, the local doctor cut off his head, claiming he wanted to test it for syphilis. Rumor had it, though, that the physician was into voodoo and witchcraft, and he wanted to use the skull in satanic rites. Whatever the reason, Joe was reburied without his noggin, and no one is really sure what became of it. Perhaps that's why Hootch Simpson's phantom is headless when it returns to prowl what's left of

Skidoo. It's said that the spectre most often shows up on evenings when there's a quarter moon, so plan accordingly.

If you're staying several days in Death Valley National Park, Amargosa Opera House and Hotel in Death Valley Junction serves as a perfect base of operations. It also has the advantage of having many resident ghosts:

- Room 9 is home to a spectre that never appears but is believed to be a child. The spirit turns doorknobs, laughs, and plays harmless pranks on guests.
- Room 24 has the ghost of a male child that drowned in the bathtub in 1976. He doesn't materialize, but residents hear him crying.
- Room 34 is the residence of an early borax miner who was murdered in the room.
- Spooky Hollow was formerly used as a morgue. No guests are allowed inside, and management won't discuss the room. It supposedly has the most paranormal activity in the building.

The theater is haunted as well. Eerie shadows cross the stage. A ghost cat has been seen throughout the playhouse and has even interrupted performances, especially those in which the owner, Martha Becket, performed. Thomas J. Willett, a former stage manager, master of ceremonies, and actor, passed away in 2005, but apparently he wasn't ready for his final curtain. His apparition has been seen sitting in the theater auditorium, watching shows.

Haunted Trails

Barker Ranch

The ruins of Barker Ranch are currently surrounded by a fence. Although they can be viewed, they can't be entered. The hike to the property basically follows the Goler Wash Road, a 4x4 drive, from the valley floor. The out-and-back hike is lightly trafficked. The difficulty is moderate to hard, based primarily on that day's heat and dust as well as the 1,600-foot change in elevation climbing up to the ranch. The trailhead and distance of the hike depend on how far you care to drive up Goler Wash Road before setting out on foot. **Barker Ranch GPS: N35 51.633' / W117 05.304'**

As you near the old ranch site, there are multiple forks in the road, and there is no cell phone service, so plan your route carefully in advance. Use a map in addition to your GPS, and ask for information and current weather conditions at one of the ranger stations. The canyon is prone to flash floods, as is all of Death Valley National Park.

There is a Death Valley National Park Information Center with parking adjacent to Hells Gate. Rangers there can give you the most accurate directions to the haunted ranch house's scorched remains. **Information Center GPS: N36 43.465' / W116 58.678'**

Devils Hole

Much of Wingate Valley is part of the China Lake Naval Weapons Center, and advance permission is required to visit. The cavern and rock formations around the mouth of Devils Hole are located very close to Ash Mountain National Wildlife Refuge in the Nevada portion of Death Valley National Park. **Devils Hole GPS: N36 25.522' / W116 17.486'**

A paved road from Spring Meadows Drive leads to the main foot trail to the cave. **Trailhead GPS: N36 25.395' / W116 18.372'**

Racetrack Grandstand and Playa

Begin your drive to Racktrack Playa at Ubehebe Crater. Head toward Teakettle Junction. You'll reach it in about 20 miles. Ignore the road to the left, which heads to Hidden Valley. Continue straight on Racetrack Valley Road to reach the Racetrack. Twenty-six miles from Ubehebe Crater, you'll reach the Grandstand, a large quartz outcrop at the north end of the Racetrack overlooking the entire playa. Park in the Grandstand parking lot and walk up the short trail to the lookout for a spectacular view. **Grandstand GPS: N36 43.465' / W116 58.678'**

If you want see the dried lakebed from an even higher elevation, take the old miner's trail up Ubehebe Peak. The path begins on the west side of the Grandstand parking lot and is 6 miles out and back. This is a difficult hike, and you'll most likely have it all to yourself.

To see the boulders on the playa up close, drive back 2 miles on Racetrack Valley Road from the direction you came. Park on the shoulder, and walk about 0.5 mile to the southeast corner of the lakebed. Remember: Don't move or remove any of the rocks. Don't deface them. And don't walk up to the rocks if it's recently rained. You'll leave behind footprints that, when dry, can last for years and detract from a future visitor's experience.

The road to Racetrack Playa is rough. A 4x4 drive, high clearance, and good tires are usually required. Off-road driving is prohibited, and there's no cell phone coverage in that part of the park. The drive time from Furnace Creek is at least 3.5 hours each way. Take plenty of fuel, and be prepared should your vehicle break down and you become stranded overnight.

Skidoo

The road out to the Skidoo ghost town is an easy, lightly trafficked 17.2-mile out-and-back hike. The trailhead is off Emigrant Canyon Road. **Trailhead GPS: N36 23.152' / W117 09.056'**

Amargosa Opera House and Hotel

Check in advance for reservations at the Amargosa Opera House and Hotel.

Amargosa Opera House and Hotel
608 Death Valley Junction
Death Valley, CA 922328
(760) 852-4441

In addition to those mentioned, there are numerous hikes possible in Death Valley National Park, some marked, most not. Always remember that conditions in the park are extreme. Take water, water, and more water. Dehydration or heat stroke can come on suddenly and be severe, even fatal. Well-broken-in hiking shoes are a must. It's recommended that you never travel alone, and always let others know what part of the valley you're planning to hike. Cell phone reception is sketchy or nonexistent in many places. Distances are vast, but because of clear, dry air, destinations can look much closer than they actually are. Finally, don't overestimate your abilities. The scenic rewards are worth the effort, but never forget the national park's name, if only as a gentle reminder to plan and prepare adequately.

Bay Area

1 Camp Tamarancho Loop Trail,
Tamarancho Trail, Camp Bothin
Fairfax

2 Alamere Falls
Bolinas

3 Dawn Falls Trail
Larkspur

4 Black Diamond Mines Regional Preserve,
Rose Hill Cemetery, Nortonville and
Black Diamond Loop, Black Diamond
Mines Loop Trail, Empire Mine Road Trail
Antioch

Marin

Contra Costa

San Francisco

Alameda

San
Mateo

Santa
Cruz

5 Perimeter Trail, Sunset Trail
to Mount Livermore,
North Ridge Trail to Mount Livermore
Angel Island State Park

6 Stow Lake, Golden Gate Park, Sutro Baths,
Golden Gate National Recreation Area
San Francisco

7 Greenbelt Trails
Hayward

8 Wilder Ranch State Park
Santa Cruz

9 The Forest of Nisene Marks State Park
Aptos

15

The Waterfall Wraiths

Alamere Falls
Bolinas, Marin County

SOMETIMES YOU WANT to get away from it all, but not *too* far away. For San Franciscans, Phillip Burton Wilderness in Marin County is a perfect choice. Lying about 20 miles northwest of the city at the southern end of Point Reyes National Seashore, its 33,000-plus forested acres have more than 100 miles of trails for day use. In addition, there are stunning seaside cliffs, many with sea caves or sandy beaches at their base. For the adventurous, leaving the established paths is allowed, but hikers do so at their own risk. The woods are full of poison oak and stinging nettle, so long pants and sleeves are highly recommended. Overnight stays in the wilderness are possible but require a permit. Hikers have a choice of four trail camps: Coast, Glen, Sky, and Wildcat.

Originally called Point Reyes Wilderness when it was established in 1976, the forest received its current name in 1985 to honor Phillip Burton, a US representative from California. Burton championed parklands throughout the state and was instrumental in the creation of the Golden Gate National Recreation Area.

Most ghost hunters hike through Phillip Burton Wilderness to visit Alamere Falls. Located on the Pacific coast, the cascade plunges 20 to 30 feet over the side of a ridge onto a narrow stretch of sand called Alamere Creek Beach before draining into the sea. Slightly upstream from the waterfall, there are three smaller cascades collectively known as the Upper Alamere Falls.

Folklore says that back in the nineteenth century, two Miwok warriors revealed their tribe's location to settlers who were hell-bent on removing all Native Americans from the region. In exchange for the information, the pioneers gave the two informants alcohol and prostitutes. For some reason, after the traitorous men's deaths, their spirits returned to Alamere Falls, where they now reside inside the plummeting waters.

Regardless of how you reach the waterfall, you may want to think twice about stepping under the spray or wading into the pool at the bottom. Those who do often report being grabbed by invisible hands, presumably one or both of the spectral warriors. Some people have had the spectres try to drown them by forcing water down their throats. Sometimes the intended victims also hear the phantoms' malicious laughter emanating from the falls.

Haunted Trails

There are multiple trails of varying length and difficulty throughout the Phillip Burton Wilderness, and several of them can get you to the crest of Alamere Falls. **Waterfall Crest GPS: N37 57.200' / W122 46.987'**

The National Park Service maintains all of the paths, and the routes are signposted. The longest single trail through the wilderness is probably the 28.5-mile Point Reyes Extended Loop, with four backpacker camps along the way. Most of the path is lightly trafficked, and its difficulty is hard. **Trailhead GPS: N38 02.367' / W122 47.987'**

If your time is limited, the best overland route to get to the falls is via the Coast Trail. The out-and-back 8.8-mile hike is of moderate difficulty and is heavily traveled. Start your walk at the Palomarin trailhead, which can be accessed from a parking lot a few miles northwest of Bolinas at the end of Mesa Road. **Palomarin Trailhead GPS: N37 56.104' / W122 44.940'**

Soon after you start your hike, the path will split with the Palomarin Trail, veering to your left. Continue straight onto the Coast Trail instead. There are great views of the Pacific all along this route, but there's a particularly nice outlook at **N37 56.262' / W121 45.720'.**

A little farther down the path—about 2.5 miles from the trailhead—you'll pass two small bodies of water. The first is Bass Lake. A short connector from the Coast Trail leads down to its shore. **Bass Lake GPS: N37 57.121' / W122 45.769'**

If you stay on the main trail instead, there's a scenic view of Pelican Lake in about 0.3 mile. **Viewpoint GPS: N37 57.125' / W122 46.392'**

There's a connector trail from the viewpoint if you want to visit the lake. **Pelican Lake GPS: N37 57.303' / W122 46.559'**

Continuing on Coast Trail, you'll next reach the highest of the three Upper Alamere Falls. **Upper Falls GPS: N37 57.244' / W122 47.268'**

Cross over Alamere Creek, which feeds all of the falls, and stay on the main trail. This will take you past the other two Upper Alamere Falls. You will soon come to the top of Alamere Falls itself at the cliff's edge. There is usually an unmarked trail visible to your right that will take you down to the beach. It's very steep and often slippery and unstable, so use extreme caution.

Make the descent *only* if you find an established trail. Do *not* scramble down the wall of the cliff just anywhere to reach the base. The ridge is mostly shale rock, which can easily splinter and crumble underfoot without warning. **Base of Alamere Falls GPS: N37 57.200' / W122 46.872'**

Whether you come down from the crest or hike along the beach to reach the waterfall, be very aware of your timing. At high tide, much of the beach is covered, and any exposed rock will be extremely slick. You don't want to be swept out to sea, get caught in a riptide, and become a ghost yourself!

16

The Shadow People

Camp Tamarancho Loop Trail, Tamarancho Trail, Camp Bothin
Fairfax, Marin County

CAMP TAMARANCHO, OWNED and operated by the Marin Council of the Boy Scouts of America, is located in the White Hill Open Space Preserve, about 25 miles northwest of San Francisco just outside the town of Fairfax.

With more than 480 acres at its disposal, the camp offers year-round wilderness activities to the public, including trails for hiking and mountain biking. The council administers the permits and fees required to use the trails, and the paths are maintained by both Scouts and a host of volunteers.

Camp Tamarancho Loop Trail circles the perimeter of the property. Enormous boulders line the path, and many of them have fallen loose and endangered bikers and backpackers over the years. Some people believe the rocks are being pushed by "shadow people," whose dark forms have been seen darting among the giant stones. Even when the mysterious creatures aren't seen, people sometimes hear their eerie whistling. These incidents usually occur in late afternoon or at dusk.

Some folks have posited that the human nightshades may be revenants of the region's indigenous inhabitants, the Coast Miwok. These Native Americans were the second largest group of Miwok, numbering in the thousands, and at one time there were more than 600 Miwok villages between the Pacific Ocean and San Pablo Bay. In fact, Marin County, where Tamarancho Trail is located, may be named for Chief Marin (native name, Huicmuse), who led the Licatiut tribe of the Miwok.

Other people think the mysterious silhouettes on the Tamarancho Trail are the ghosts of early European explorers or apparitions of American pioneers who migrated from back East. Of course there's always the possibility that they could be some sort of cryptid or different paranormal presence entirely.

Who and what these shadowy entities actually are—and whether they're living or dead—is unknown, so any attempt to identify them is pure conjecture. Nor is any reason known why they chose to "haunt" the Tamarancho Trail. Fortunately, there have been no reports of rocks hitting anyone on the trail, so maybe the shadow people aren't as dangerous as the old wives' tales suggest.

The Girl Scouts have their own campground nearby, Camp Bothin. Before the camp was established, the property held a convalescent home for women and children. Started by Henry E. Bothin in 1905, the rest home operated there until 1940. A tubercular hospital remained on the site until the 1950s. Starting in 1948, the Marin Girl Scouts Council was allowed to use portions of the property for summer activities. Every year the number of projects and campers grew until, in 1959, the entire property was leased to the Girl Scouts. Though known as Camp Bothin, the site is officially the Henry E. Bothin Youth Center.

Of course before all of that, Native Americans inhabited the region, and legend has it the local tribes considered the land where Camp Bothin now stands to be sacred.

The local hiking trails aren't said to be haunted, but there's plenty of spooky stuff going on in the campground itself. Ghosts of Native Americans in tribal garb pop up everywhere on the property. They're frightening but harmless. The disembodied cries of former patients are heard in all of the old hospital buildings, and phantom nurses still make their rounds in the halls. Now and then, apparitions from both time periods materialize at the same time, oblivious to each other's presence.

Haunted Trails

Camp Tamarancho Loop Trail is a moderate-difficulty 6.2-mile trek with moderate traffic. The route was designed as a singletrack course for mountain bikes, but hikers are also welcome. In recent years, a few parts of the path have been widened with a second bike lane. Much of the trail is shaded, which is particularly welcome during the summer months, but the tracks can be rough going after a heavy rain. There's also the matter of a 1,500-foot elevation gain over the course of the hike, with many steep switchbacks on the sometimes-narrow path. **Trailhead GPS: N37 59.663' / W122 36.494'**

The loop can also be accessed by a separate path about 3 miles to the north, outside of camp property but still within the White Hill Open Space Preserve. By setting out from there, the Tamarancho Trail hike becomes a 9.9-mile loop. This additional section of the path is more difficult than the rest, changing the trail's overall rating to hard. **Trailhead Extension GPS: N38 00.566' / W122 37.031'**

17

The Dawn Falls Vampire

Dawn Falls Trail
Larkspur, Marin County

DAWN FALLS ARE located within the 639-acre Blithedale Summit Open Space Preserve, just outside Larkspur in Marin County. The park contains a variety of flora, from chaparral and lush ferns to dense forests, including groves of redwood. Almost all of its pathways are shaded.

The short hike to the cascades would be a worry-free walk if it weren't for the possibility of running into an enigmatic female fiend that roams Dawn Falls Trail. Though she's sometimes described as a witch, what worries hikers is her fiendish thirst for blood—especially from men.

At first the backpacker sees no one else on the path, but he feels a sudden chill and a growing sense of apprehension. He then spots a stranger far ahead on the trail. Even from a distance, her look is striking: an attractive face, long black hair, and trendy "Goth" attire. As the unsuspecting hiker approaches her, however, the woman's appearance transforms into that of a hideous hag, her hair now stringy and wild. And most terrifying of all, when she parts her lips, a set of long, gleaming fangs is exposed.

Needless to say, those who see the nightmarish creature immediately turn and run. Most people escape unharmed, but the vixen has been known to leap onto a hiker's back as he flees and sink her teeth into his neck. The victim can feel the vampire's weight and the blood trickling from his throat. Eventually, he reaches the trailhead or meets others on the path. Only then does he realize the hellish harpy is no longer there. Just as surprising, there are no punctures marks on his neck or any sign of blood.

Local legend provides no backstory or explanation for the mysterious old crone.

Haunted Trails

Dawn Falls can be accessed via an easy, moderately trafficked 2.2-mile out-and-back hike. The kid-friendly pathway is even and fairly flat, with only a slight rise as you approach the falls. Dawn Falls Trail begins at the end of Madrone Avenue, and parking is very limited. The best time to visit is April through midsummer (or after a heavy rain), when the cascades and the creek that feeds them are at their peak. **Trailhead GPS: N37 55.862' / W122 33.050'**

Many people continue on the trail past Dawn Falls and return by way of a marked path through Baltimore Canyon, thus creating a 2.7-mile loop trail of moderate difficulty. If you're even more ambitious, it's possible to put together a 4.4-mile loop trail of moderate difficulty by starting your hike at the Piedmont trailhead. Parking is limited. **Piedmont Trailhead GPS: N37 55.703' / W122 32.312'**

About 0.8 mile into the walk, Piedmont Trail meets the Dawn Falls Trail at the Madrone Intersection. After viewing the waterfall, continue through Baltimore Canyon to complete the loop. **Madrone Intersection GPS: N37 55.825' / W122 33.067'**

18

The Ellis Island of the West

*Perimeter Trail, Sunset Trail to Mount Livermore, North Ridge
Trail to Mount Livermore*
Angel Island State Park, Marin County

LMOST ALL AMERICANS have heard of Ellis Island in New York City, which processed more than 12 million European immigrants from 1892 to 1954. Fewer people know about Angel Island in San Francisco Bay, which operated as a major West Coast immigration station from 1910 to 1940.

The first people to set foot on the 760-acre island were the Coast Miwok. They didn't build permanent villages, but they visited frequently and set up camp while fishing and hunting. The first European visitors were under the command of Lt. Juan Manuel de Ayala, a Spanish navigator who sailed his ship, the *San Carlos*, into what is now Ayala Cove. He named the island Isla de Los Angeles, meaning Island of the Angels, or Angel Island.

Because of its strategic location, the US Army established Camp Reynolds on Angel Island in 1863. Its original mission was to protect the Bay Area during the Civil War, but it was later used as a base of operations during the western wars against the Native Americans. Just before the turn of the twentieth century, the army renamed the whole island Fort McDowell. Camp Reynolds became the West Garrison, and an East Garrison was established at Quarry Point.

During World War I, East Garrison acted as an army recruitment center as well as a processing station to discharge returning soldiers. Later it was an embarkation site for soldiers heading to the Pacific theater during World War II. With no postwar need for the island, the army deemed it surplus property and departed in 1946.

Their withdrawal didn't last long. In 1954, in the early days of the Cold War, the army returned to install a Nike missile launch site. By 1962 the weapons had become outdated, so the army once again left Angel Island. With the exception of a few active facilities operated by the US Coast Guard, the island was ceded to the California State Parks system in 1963.

In 1891 a quarantine station had been set up at Ayala Cove (then known as Hospital Cove), where immigrants were held in isolation if it was suspected they were carrying disease. Entire ships could be held in the cove if necessary. In time, more effective treatment operations became available, and the Angel Island Quarantine Station was closed in 1946.

More important to our ghost story is the US Immigration Station. Almost a million people from more than eighty countries arrived by sea and were processed at this "Guardian of the Western Gate." First-class passengers and European immigrants were quickly processed onboard before they disembarked.

Chinese immigrants, however, were not allowed to settle in the United States due to the Chinese Exclusion Act of 1882. Nevertheless, about 175,000 Chinese arrived at Angel Island, hoping to be granted entry. In the end, most of the immigrants were allowed to stay in the United States, but it was a long and grueling process.

Those under detention faced uncertainty and endured loneliness, despair, and constant humiliation. Though meals were provided, malnutrition was widespread. Several of the Chinese documented their ordeals by writing forlorn messages on the walls of their barracks or carving them into the wooden slats. A few wrote long, heartbreaking poems.

Some of the immigrants succumbed to disease while in quarantine. A few committed suicide, unable to bear the indignity of being confined merely because of their ancestry. These restless dead are among the numerous spirits that haunt the island. Modern-day visitors to Angel Island have seen restless apparitions with Asian features and wearing period wardrobe. They're spotted inside the old detention barracks or roaming the trails. A few folks have claimed they were attacked by unseen spectres. One angry ghost is said to assault females of any age, sometimes by pressing on their chests and making it difficult for them to breathe.

Why visit Angel Island these days? For hikers, its trails provide stunning views of San Francisco Bay, Alcatraz, and the Golden Gate and Bay Bridges. Several of the paths lead to the top of 778-foot Mount Livermore, the highest point on the island. The hill was named for Caroline Livermore, the conservationist whose work was largely responsible for Angel Island being declared a state park.

History buffs visit the former immigration station located in China Cove on the isle's northern coast. A fire razed the administration building in 1940, but some of the detention barracks survived. The entire property is now a museum, and the barracks hold enlightening displays that include personal effects of some of the detainees. Restorations have provided a vivid re-creation of the residents' living space and conditions.

And then there are visitors who come just for the ghosts.

Haunted Trails

There are three major trails on Angel Island. Perimeter Trail is an easy, heavily trafficked 5.9-mile hike. It mostly follows Perimeter Road, which is paved and even, although there are a couple of rises that can be mildly tiring. If you set out clockwise, you'll reach the Angel Island Immigration Station about 1.5 miles into your walk. **Trailhead GPS: N37 52.116' / W122 26.078'**

The Sunset Trail to Mount Livermore is an easy 4.6-mile out-and-back hike with moderate traffic. There is an elevation gain of 656 feet. **Trailhead GPS: N37 51.892' / W122 25.962'**

The North Ridge Trail to Mount Livermore is 4 miles long. It's an easy out-and-back walk with moderate traffic. The hike starts with a climb of 144 stairs that lead to Perimeter Road. **Trailhead GPS: N37 52.121' / W122 19.471'**

There are also many connector paths between the larger trails. For example, the Sunset and North Ridge Trails meet about 0.3 mile from the top of Mount Livermore, so you could create a loop hike by taking one route up and the other back down. All of the island's trails are kid friendly.

Travel to Angel Island is by ferry, either from Pier 41 in San Francisco via the Blue and Gold Fleet (blueandgoldfleet.com/ferry/angel-island/) or from the town of Tiburon across the bay (angelislandferry.com). The former's route passes closer to Alcatraz and takes a bit longer to get to Angel Island, and it's slightly more expensive. The number of ferries each day is limited, and their times change seasonally. Plan carefully.

All ferries arrive at Ayala Cove. There you'll find a modest visitor center that offers informative exhibits illuminating the story of Angel Island, as well as free maps.

The cove also has a small cafe and a general store, but food and other concessions on the island are expensive. Guided nature walks, tram excursions, and Segway tours set out from the cove, and there are bike rentals available. If you plan to cycle, you may want to bring your own bike or rent one in San Francisco or Tiburon.

The museum and barracks of the former immigration station are open for visitors Wednesday through Sunday, 11 a.m. to 3 p.m., subject to change. There is an admission fee for those 6 and older. The museum offers guided tours daily for a slight additional fee. The Angel Island Immigration Station Foundation has posted an exceptional video showing highlights from the museum and its tour at youtube.com/watch?v=ZnpgiUY5ip4.

For those who want to stay on Angel Island overnight, there are eleven campsites around the island, each of which can accommodate eight people. All of the sites have running water, toilets, food lockers, and charcoal barbecues. (Wood fires are prohibited anywhere on the island.)

Reservations are essential. Make them by calling the California Department of Parks and Recreation at (800) 444-7275 or online at parks.ca.gov or reserveamerica.com. Book as far in advance as possible, especially for the summer months or if you want a particular campground.

19

The Ghosts of Golden Gate Park

Stow Lake, Golden Gate Park, Sutro Baths, Golden Gate National Recreation Area
San Francisco, San Francisco County

I T'S EASY TO leave your heart in San Francisco. At least two folks have also left their spirits behind in the city's largest recreational area, Golden Gate Park. And why not? If you want to spend your afterlife in beautiful but urban surroundings, it doesn't get much nicer than Golden Gate Park.

Located on 1,017 acres on the west side of San Francisco, Golden Gate Park is more than 3 miles long and about 0.5 mile wide. Like Manhattan's Central Park, it's rectangular in shape, only 20 percent larger. (Golden Gate Park isn't a perfect rectangle, however, because it has an 8-block narrow strip of land known as the Panhandle extending to the east.)

Calls for the creation of a grand, public recreational space in the Bay Area began in the 1860s, and it was determined that the best place for it would be on what were called the Outside Lands—an expanse of sandy soil and shore dunes between downtown and the sea.

Noted engineer William Hammond Hall surveyed the donated property and plotted the proposed site in 1870. The following year, he was appointed commissioner of the San Francisco Recreation and Parks

Department, which was established to oversee the park's completion and to administer it once it was opened.

John McLaren was hired as the master gardener, and he began by planting bent grass and trees in the dunes to stabilize them. By 1875 more than 150,000 trees had been added to the property, including several species new to California. And that was just the beginning. Carefully cultivated grasses, ferns, shrubbery, flowers, and other flora soon dotted the park. Paved and dirt trails were laid, crisscrossing the grounds. Two major roads were added for motorized traffic, John F. Kennedy Drive and Martin Luther King Jr. Drive, along with a handful of minor streets and twenty-one entrances for those driving into the park.

Attractions in the park include the Japanese Tea Garden, the Conservatory of Flowers, the California Academy of Sciences, the De Young Museum, the San Francisco Botanical Garden at Strybing Arboretum, the Shakespeare Garden, a carousel, playing fields for various sports, two windmills, and even a paddock housing bison. Access to the park is free, but there's an admission charge to some of the museums and gardens.

There are also almost a dozen lakes of various shapes and sizes landscaped into Golden Gate Park. The most important one to ghost enthusiasts is Stow Lake, which contains a few small islets and a large tree-filled island called Strawberry Hill. A peninsula before it was encircled by water, Strawberry Hill is home to the park's first artificial waterfall. Named Huntingdon Waterfall, the cascade is fed by a reservoir on the top of the island. Strawberry Hill can be reached by two bridges, Roman Bridge on the north side or Stone (also called Rustic) Bridge to the south. For those so inclined, rowboats and paddleboats can be rented at the lakeside boathouse.

Which brings us to our first ghost story. Legend has it that one day in the late nineteenth or early twentieth century a young mother, dressed in a swimsuit of the era, was in a rowboat on Stow Lake with her baby. The infant accidentally fell overboard, and the woman dove into the water to try to save the child. Both drowned.

Like all long-standing tales, there are several variations. One says that the woman had managed to hide her pregnancy and delivered the baby without anyone's knowledge. She killed the infant herself—it's unclear whether she disposed of the child in the lake or elsewhere—and then, in remorse, committed suicide by drowning herself in the lake. In another version, the mother threw herself into the reservoir atop Strawberry Hill instead of the lake.

There's an even spookier telling of the story. In that account, the woman and baby were floating blissfully in the rowboat when, out of nowhere, an unidentifiable shriek was heard. Almost immediately, some unknown entity reached out of the water, yanked the baby from the boat, and dragged the infant under. Here, too, the mother leapt in to save her child, but both she and the baby drowned.

People claim that the woman's ghost now walks around Stow Lake searching for her baby. She even talks to passersby, asking them whether they've seen the child. The spectre has been described as being soaking wet and having long, stringy hair and a grief-stricken face.

If you're impatient for the woman's spirit to appear on its own, it's said you're able to summon it by chanting "White lady, white lady, I have your baby" three times in a row. Supposedly, you'll be most successful calling up the spirit if you stand next to the Pioneer Women and Children statue on the lake's north side. (Some say the sculpture itself is haunted and that the expressions on the statue's faces change at night.)

Before you conjure the female phantom, though, carefully consider what could happen if she does materialize. According to an old wives' tale, if you admit you don't have the baby, the spectre will pull you into the lake and drown you in anger. If she thinks you actually might have the infant but are simply hiding it, she'll haunt you for the rest of your life.

The *San Francisco Chronicle* suggests that the basis for the myth is a 1906 report that some children found a drowned baby in the lake. How much of the ensuing ghost story is true is anyone's guess.

There's another spirit haunting Golden Gate Park, a phantom policeman, but he doesn't interact with hikers. Instead, he pulls over speeding cars and issues tickets to the drivers. But here's the insane part: When you later try to pay the fine, the city says it has no officer by that name—or if it did, he had died a decade earlier. Interestingly, the ghost seems to be bound to the park, because when he tries to leave it, he and the patrol car disappear.

All things considered, if you bump into the phantom woman or the ethereal policeman during a visit to Golden Gate Park, be careful how you interact. There's plenty to see and do without having to deal with the Other Side.

The Sutro Baths was a huge saltwater swimming pool and recreation center built by wealthy businessman and former San Francisco mayor Adolph Sutro. (Cliff House, Sutro's luxurious private residence, dominated the bluff above the facility. The mansion currently operates as a restaurant.) Opened in 1896, the swimming complex was located just a few blocks north of Golden Gate Park, and an electric trolley line linked the two. The Baths had six pools of varying sizes, more than 500 dressing rooms, a museum containing natural and historical artifacts, and an amphitheater. Water was circulated in and out of the pools from the ocean, by pump at low tide and naturally at high tide.

There was initially great public interest in the Sutro Baths, but, for whatever reason, the water park never really caught on. With ever-rising maintenance costs and after years of declining business, including an ill-fated attempt to convert the place into an ice-skating rink, Sutro Baths finally closed. The property was sold to real estate developers in 1964. Two years later, a fire, later determined to be the result of arson, tore through the buildings while the site was being demolished. Many of the crumbling foundations and some of the broken walls were never removed and remain in place. Today the property is part of the Golden Gate National Recreation Area, and visitors are free to climb over what's left of the Sutro Baths.

Nighttime hikers have reported seeing apparitions of former patrons of the baths cavorting among the ruins as if the buildings were still standing. The ghosts are easily recognizable by their early twentieth-century swimwear and period wardrobe. The spirits can even be faintly heard laughing, singing, hobnobbing with one another, and frolicking in and alongside the long-gone pools.

Urban folklore says that Satanists, perhaps even members of Anton LaVey's San Francisco–based Church of Satan, occasionally practiced rituals (including human sacrifice) in and around the passageway of an adjacent sea cave. Supposedly, if you go at dusk and place a lit candle at the opening of the tunnel on the ocean side, an invisible hand—possibly belonging to one of the cult's victims—will pick it up and throw it into the sea. An alternate version of the old wives' tale says that if you leave the lit candle outside the cave before you enter, it'll be gone when you return. (There's always a slight danger of a powerful, unexpected wave splashing into the cave. Use extreme caution if decide to go inside.)

Haunted Trails

Golden Gate Park
While there are lots of trails to choose from in Golden Gate Park, your best chance of running into the spectral mother is on the Stow Lake and Strawberry Hill Loop. It's an easy, heavily trafficked 2 miles. This distance includes the walk around the lake's perimeter, which is fairly level and even, and a visit to Strawberry Hill and Huntington Falls. Although the hike could start anywhere along the water's edge, the nominal trailhead is next to the lake's boathouse. **Trailhead GPS: N37 46.244' / W122 28.642'**

Another path that takes in more of the park is the easy, heavily trafficked Golden Gate Park Trail. The route is a 6.1-mile loop. It passes Stow Lake twice but doesn't completely circle it. **Trailhead GPS: N37 45.984' / W122 27.958'**

Finally, Golden Gate Park Perimeter Loop stretches almost the entire length of the park, including much of its border. Most people who take this 7.3-mile moderate hike recommend doing the loop clockwise. The trail doesn't circle Stow Lake completely, but it runs along its eastern edge for about 0.3 mile. **Trailhead GPS: N37 46.203' / W122 30.636'**

Sutro Baths

An easy to moderate 0.6-mile, heavily trafficked loop trail descends from a parking area into the ruins of Sutro Baths. Dogs are allowed but must be kept on a leash. **Trailhead GPS: N37 46.827' / W122 30.708'**

20

The Wailing Witch

*Black Diamond Mines Regional Preserve, Rose Hill Cemetery,
Nortonville and Black Diamond Loop, Black Diamond Mines Loop
Trail, Empire Mine Road Trail*
Antioch, Contra Costa County

I N THE NINETEENTH century, coal was a major fuel, and a reliable, inexpensive source was needed for the settlers and businesses streaming into California. As luck would have it, one was discovered in the 1850s about 40 miles from San Francisco in the hills south of Antioch.

The whole area became known collectively as the Mount Diablo Coalfield due to its location a few miles northeast of the mountain, but there were twelve separate mines in operation: Black Diamond, Central, Corcoran, Cumberland, Empire, Eureka, Star, Independent, Manhattan, Mt. Hope, Pittsburg, and Union. Numerous small towns sprang up to work them, but almost all of them are now ghost towns. Nortonville was the first and largest of the communities, at one time having a population of about 1,000 people.

Unfortunately, the coal was very low quality, and by the turn of the twentieth century it became affordable to import a better grade of coal from the East. The nail in the coffin for the mines was the rise of the gas and petroleum industries. After the mines closed, there were few local jobs available, and folks left the region. Almost overnight, the towns were empty, and the land returned to cattle grazing. Many years later, mining did start again briefly, but it was for the fine silica used in glassmaking rather than coal.

In 1973 the East Bay Regional Park District acquired the coalfields and turned them into the 6,000-acre Black Diamond Mines Regional Preserve. Although the shafts of the coal mines have been sealed for safety reasons, a few feet of some of their entryways have been kept open so that visitors can take a peek inside. Rangers give guided tours of one of the sand mines, and there are open-air remnants of three ghost towns. On top of that, there are 60 miles of established hiking trails.

The park is home to two ghosts, one of which is known as the Wailing Witch. According to legend, the apparition was a townswoman entrusted with the care of several children who mysteriously died one by one. She was accused of witchcraft, found guilty, and summarily executed.

Details of the actual historical events remain sketchy, but the story does have a basis in fact. The woman's name was most likely Mary. She was the schoolteacher for the mining towns, so naturally she spent a great deal of time with the residents' youngsters. As for their illnesses, they weren't caused by spells. In the late 1800s, diphtheria, scarlet fever, smallpox, and typhoid all swept through the communities, and the students probably succumbed during one of the outbreaks. Mary was tried and put to death, despite her being innocent of sorcery.

The Wailing Witch's burial place is unknown, and her last name is forgotten, but she occasionally shows up at the entrances to the mines. Though frightening, she's there to warn people, not to scare them: There are harmful gases in the mines, and the tunnels are unstable and dangerous. It's mostly children who see Mary, but over the years she's manifested to folks of all ages. She's never been known to hurt anyone, but she will forcefully push people out of the mine if she must. She's also been known to gently tug at youngsters' hair to stop them from going farther inside.

The other phantom, Sarah Norton, is eternally tied to Rose Hill Cemetery. Located within Black Diamond Mines Regional Preserve, the

1-acre graveyard is the final resting place for some of the people who lived on the Mount Diablo Coalfield. It's believed that there were more than 200 interments in the burial ground, but there are only about eighty markers remaining in the cemetery. Many of the gravesites had wooden markers, which quickly rotted or became victims of vandalism and theft.

One of still-identifiable graves belongs to Sarah Norton, the wife of Noah Norton, who founded Nortonville. She was a popular midwife and delivered more than 600 babies. Sarah died in 1879 at the age of 68 when she was tossed from her carriage on the way to make yet another delivery. (Some sources say the buggy overturned and crushed her.)

Sarah's family knew that she didn't want a church funeral, but she was so beloved that local townsfolk insisted on giving her one anyway. The day of the service an unexpected storm blew through the area, so the ceremony was postponed overnight. Astonishingly, an even more violent gale whipped up the next day—so strong that cattle stampeded. The townspeople conceded defeat and buried Sarah without fanfare in Rose Hill Cemetery. Could the displeasure of Sarah's spirit have caused the tempests? It's impossible to know. Regardless, she hasn't taken her burial lying down. Her ghost, sometimes called the White Witch, frequently floats among the few markers in Rose Hill Cemetery at night, and she also strolls over the nearby hills.

By the way, Sarah's apparition isn't the only paranormal activity in the graveyard. There are unexplainable audible oddities too. People have reported hearing a nonexistent bell tolling and the sound of crying and laughter.

We can't leave Antioch without mentioning Empire Mine Road Trail. Formerly a two-lane highway, the street has been closed to vehicular traffic for more than a decade. The route is lined with green fields, rolling hills, and, in season, wildflowers, but many paranormal buffs walk the path to see the so-called "Gates of Hell."

Despite its devilish name, the wood-and-metal fence along Empire Mine Road looks much like an ordinary farm fence used to hold in livestock—except one of its gates is locked and blocked by two heavy concrete traffic barricades to prevent anyone from turning onto a particular side street. Local folklore says there's an abandoned building at the end of the lane and that intense, negative auras left over from its days as an insane asylum have opened a portal to the netherworld.

There's also a deserted slaughterhouse on the way to the closed asylum that's allegedly haunted by the spectre of an old man. The road has its own apparition: a female phantom floating above the pavement holding a knife. She's thought to be the angry spirit of a woman who fatally stabbed her ex-boyfriend on the lane in 1995. He somehow managed to stagger back onto Empire Mine Road, where he was later found dead, covered in blood.

Empire Mine Road Trail is open to hikers, but the Gates of Hell, the side road, and all of the surrounding land are private property. Yes, if you stray from Empire Mine Road, there could be legal ramifications, but more importantly, it might also be a life-or-death decision.

Haunted Trails

Black Diamond Mines Preserve
The 5.7-mile Nortonville and Black Diamond Loop is lightly traveled, in part because it's rated hard in difficulty. **Trailhead GPS: N37 57.517' / W121 51.802'**

From the parking area, the Nortonville Trail ascends until it reaches Rose Hill Cemetery. After visiting the graveyard, continue on the trail up and over a ridge, then drop down into what structures remain of Nortonville.

You could return at this point by retracing your steps, but if you want to complete the loop, head into the adjacent Coal Canyon. Once there, take the turnoff on your left onto the paved Black Diamond Trail. At the closed gate at the top of the hill, turn left onto the dirt track, which is also part of Black Diamond Trail. This will lead you back to the Nortonville Trail.

The 5.3-mile Black Diamond Mines Loop Trail is a moderate difficulty route that covers much of the same territory, including the Rose Hill Cemetery and Nortonville. The trail is heavily trafficked and sets out from the former site of Somersville, one of the other ghost towns. **Trailhead GPS: N37 57.497' / W121 51.980'**

Black Diamond Mines Preserve is open daily from 8 a.m. until dusk. There is a nominal fee to enter the preserve. A reservation is required to set up camp for overnight stays. If you plan to duck into one of the mine entryways to look for the Wailing Witch, check with the visitor center before you begin your search. The rangers can provide maps and suggest trails that go past some of the old mines.

Empire Mine Road Trail
Empire Mine Road Trail is an easy 6.8-mile out-and-back paved walkway. **Trailhead GPS: N37 57.537' / W121 48.284'**

21

Murder in Memorial Park

Greenbelt Trails
Hayward, Alameda County

P EOPLE FROM OUTSIDE the Bay Area can be forgiven if they hear the phrase "Hayward Plunge" and think it refers to a high rock or cliff from which local daredevils jump into a lake or river far below. The colorful moniker does refer to swimming but with a lot less risk: Hayward Plunge is a large indoor pool located in the city of Hayward on the east side of San Francisco Bay.

The pool was constructed in 1936 by the Works Progress Administration, which built public structures and roads during the Great Depression. Some eighty-plus years later, Hayward Plunge is still open and going strong. In addition to its hours for general use, the pool also offers swimming lessons, water fitness programs, adult lap sessions, and even special "tot swim" times. It's administered by the 100-square-mile Hayward Area Recreation and Park District, which was created in 1944 to provide leisure facilities for the multicity region.

But even a place designed for fun and frolic can have a dark side. The eerie occurrences at Hayward Plunge don't take place inside the building. Rather, its ghosts haunt the hiking trail out back.

According to local legend, sometime in the 1960s, a swim instructor asked a group of children he was coaching to hike a wooded path with him that started next to the pool and headed into Ward Creek Canyon.

Somewhere on the trail, at an open space overlooking the stream, the trainer murdered all of the youngsters and dumped their bodies into Ward Creek. (In one variation of the tale, the man kidnapped and bound the children instead and dragged them to the clearing to kill them.)

Ever since the horrific incident took place, people walking the pathway after dark have reported hearing phantom children crying for help. Oddly, some folks have heard their ethereal voices laughing instead. There are also disembodied footsteps, dark figures, and sudden, unexplainable cold spots. The hauntings often start within 200 yards of the trailhead.

There is no evidence to back up the Hayward Plunge ghost story, so it's impossible to point out where the murders supposedly took place on the trail. But here's some advice if you want to try to find it: Go at night—and follow the screams.

Haunted Trails

Hayward Plunge is in the Memorial Park section of the Hayward Area Recreation and Park District, and the adjacent trail is part of the signposted Greenbelt Trails system, which is made up of three separate but connected paths. Together they form a 6.3- to 7.1-mile loop, depending how many little side trails you explore. The first section is colloquially known as the Hayward Plunge Trail but is technically the Wally Wicklander Memorial Trail. It sets out from the parking lot next to Hayward Plunge and basically follows Ward Creek to the east. **Trailhead GPS: N37 39.907' / W122 04.636'**

After about 1.5 miles, the trail leaves Memorial Park, crosses Campus Drive, and enters another park, the Hayward Greenbelt. Almost immediately, the trail splits. At the fork, most hikers take Ward Creek Road Trail to the right. It eventually intersects Durham Way, which can be used as a connector path to reach East Avenue Trail. Take that path west. It will follow the north ridge of the wooded canyon until it reconnects with the Wicklander Trail. From there, retrace your steps back to Hayward Plunge.

The full hike is of moderate difficulty and, surprisingly for its suburban location, only moderately trafficked. Almost the entire route is shaded, and it's open to cyclists and leashed dogs as well as hikers.

Hayward Plunge
24176 Mission Blvd.
Hayward, CA 94544
(510) 881-6703

22

The Sinister Sisters

Wilder Ranch State Park
Santa Cruz, Santa Cruz County

The Forest of Nisene Marks State Park
Aptos, Santa Cruz County

B EFORE THE MEXICAN-AMERICAN War, which ran from 1846 to 1848, all of the land that is now California was part of Mexico. Historically, the Spanish monarchy and, later, Mexican governors made a practice of giving large swaths of property to private individuals to thank them for their services to the state.

A perfect example is the land that is today Wilder Ranch State Park. It's located along the coast at the northern end of Monterey Bay, just north of Santa Cruz. Before the arrival of Europeans, the Ohlone peoples populated the region. Spanish explorer Gaspar de Portolà passed through in 1776, and the Franciscans opened Mission Santa Cruz in 1791. The Catholic brothers established Rancho Arroyo de Matadero on the land west of their mission to raise and butcher cattle. They operated the ranch until 1835. As for the Ohlone, with their land confiscated, most of them moved away. Quite a few contracted disease from the newcomers and, having no natural immunity, died.

In 1839 Juan Bautista Alvarado, the governor of Alta California, ceded the former mission and ranch to the three daughters of José Joaquin

Castro, who had arrived during the second Spanish expedition in the late eighteenth century. The women's names were Maria Candida, Jacinta, and Maria de los Angeles, and the understanding from the governor was that each of the women would receive a third of the property.

The oldest sister, Maria Candida, had married in 1822. Little is known about her husband's past except that he was from Siberia and had left a Russian vessel as soon as it arrived in California. He immediately changed his name to José Antonio Bolcoff and became a naturalized Mexican citizen. After the land grant to Maria Candida, he built two adobes on the ranch, opened a sawmill, and also began dairy farming.

By 1839 Maria de los Angeles had also married, and Jacinta had entered a Monterey convent. Around 1850 Maria de los Angeles and her husband filed a claim for their portion of what was, by then, being called Rancho Refugio. The court denied the petition because her sister Maria Candida and her sister's husband, José, were the only ones who had legally registered themselves as the landowners. After the hearing, Bolcoff realized the ruling could be overturned if evidence were produced that the property had, indeed, been intended to be equally divided among the sisters, so he destroyed any documents that could prove their case. Then, in 1860, Bolcoff forged a bogus document that deeded the parts of the ranch that actually belonged to his sisters-in-law to his own sons.

Maria de los Angeles never forgave her eldest sister and the scheming husband. Nor did Jacinta—and she was a nun! Cheated out of what was rightfully theirs, the embittered sisters are said to have returned to haunt the property after their death. Both of their spirits are still seen walking across the open meadows as well as in the area around the old, remaining ranch houses. The ghosts never appear together. Jacinta is easily recognized because she's in her habit; Maria wears a nineteenth-century-style dress. Both of the spectres remain aloof and walk very slowly, and they never speak or turn if they're called. They both have deep-set black eyes, and Maria de los Angeles always seems to wear an expression of barely contained rage.

After the rancho had passed through several hands, California State Parks acquired much of the original property and, in 1974, renamed it Wilder Ranch State Park. It encompasses 7,000 acres between Ben Lomond Mountain and the Pacific Ocean, and it's home to a large variety of flora and fauna. The park's mandate is to preserve its historic 1840 adobe, the Victorian farmhouse, the working dairy farm, and its fields, forests, coastal cliffs, sea caves, and beaches.

The apparitions of Maria de los Angeles and Jacinta Castro still roam the fields, but the park has 34 miles of hiking trails, all of which are also open to bikers and equestrians. Locating the spectres would be like finding the proverbial needle in a haystack. But there's always hope.

Situated just 8 miles south of Santa Cruz on CA 1, the town of Aptos stretches from the Pacific shore up to The Forest of Nisene Marks State Park in the Santa Cruz Mountains. There are more than 40 miles of trails for hiking and mountain biking in the park's 10,000 acres. The woods were clear-cut by loggers between 1883 and 1923, so what's seen today is all second growth. The park is named for Nisene Marks, who bought the land from lumber interests in the 1950s. The Marks family deeded more than 9,000 acres of the property to the state to be kept as a "natural preserve" in 1963.

Several trails in The Forest of Nisene Marks State Park are lined with trees that allegedly had been used to hang women found guilty of witchcraft. Hikers have seen their apparitions dangling from tree limbs overhead, nooses still wrapped around the ghosts' necks. No specific pathways are mentioned in the legends, however, so be on guard no matter which route you take. If you spot one of the spectral witches, turn away. It's claimed that she'll lay a curse on you if you look her in the eye.

Haunted Trails

Old Landing Cove Trail. 2.3-mile loop. Easy difficulty. Light traffic. **Trailhead GPS: N36 57.614' / W122 05.156'**

Englesman Loop Trail to Wild Boar Trail. 4.5 miles. Moderate difficulty. Moderate traffic. **Trailhead GPS: N36 57.909' / W122 05.036'**

Englesman, Long Meadow, Eucalyptus, Wilder Ridge Loop. 9.6 miles. Moderate difficulty. Moderate traffic. **Trailhead GPS: N36 57.909' / W122 05.122'**

Pacific to Redwood Loop. 12 miles. Hard difficulty. Moderate to heavy traffic. **Trailhead GPS: N36 57.909' / W122 05.122'**

Wilder Ranch State Park is open daily between 8 a.m. and sunset. The visitor center is open Thursday through Sunday, 8 a.m. to 4 p.m. There is a fee for parking. If you want to try to spot the Castro sisters near the old adobe or farmhouse, ask at the center for directions to the buildings. All of the trails in Wilder Ranch State Park are popular with bikers, so be on guard if you're hiking a section of trail that's a single cycling lane.

Greater Los Angeles

1 Elings Park, Alice Keck Park Memorial Gardens, Los Prietos Campground
Santa Barbara

2 San Miguel Island, Santa Cruz Island, Santa Rosa Island
Channel Islands National Park

3 Santa Rosa Trail, Lower Butte Trail, Wildwood Mesa Trail, Teepee Trail, Wildwood Canyon Trail, Paradise Falls
Thousand Oaks

4 Hummingbird Trail
Simi Valley

5 Solstice Canyon Trail, Century Lake, Malibou Lake, Malibu Creek State Park
Malibu

6 Murphy Ranch
Pacific Palisades

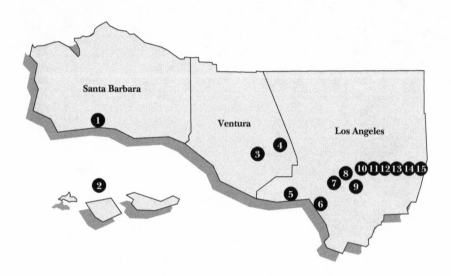

7 East Ridge Trail (Inspiration Point Walking Trail), West Ridge Trail (Western Highway Trail), Runyon Canyon Fire Road Trail, Runyon Canyon Park
West Hollywood

8 Mount Lee Drive Trail, Wonder View Trail, Hollyridge Trail, Canyon Drive Trail
Hollywood

9 Old Zoo Trail, Bee Rock Trail, Haunted Picnic Table 29, Griffith Park, Corralitas Red Car Trail
Los Angeles

10 Mount Wilson Toll Road, Eaton Canyon Trail, Eaton Canyon Falls
Pasadena

11 The Cobb Estate, Sunset Ridge Trail, Millard Canyon Falls Trail, Sam Merrill Trail to Echo Mountain, the Altadena Gravity Hill
Altadena

12 Sturtevant Falls Trail, Angeles National Forest
Arcadia

13 Monrovia Canyon Waterfall Trail
Monrovia

14 East Fork Trail of the San Gabriel River, Crystal Lake Trail, South Mount Hawkins Trail
Azusa

15 Thompson Creek Trail
Claremont

23

The Queen of Elings Park

Elings Park, Alice Keck Park Memorial Garden, Los Prietos Campground
Santa Barbara, Santa Barbara County

ELINGS PARK, LOCATED along the ocean in the southeast corner of Santa Barbara, is the largest privately funded park in the United States.

All is fun and games there during the day, but every evening brings another opportunity to encounter the park's resident ghost, the ethereal Queen Mab.

The spirit comes out to play at dusk, as temperatures drop and cool breezes begin to waft in from the ocean. Her sobriquet refers to the nighttime fairy creature mentioned in Shakespeare's *Romeo and Juliet*.

The Queen Mab of Elings Park was once a flesh-and-blood human being, however. Her ghost seldom materializes, but visitors hear her. At first they think the sound is merely the rustle of leaves or a gust of wind. But then they realize it's a soft, disembodied female voice whispering in their ear. The spectre confesses secrets from her sorrowful past, but the details only come in small snippets. According to some people who have heard her, Queen Mab may have killed someone or been a murder victim herself.

Locals were aware of the ethereal lady long before the establishment of Elings Park. They also knew that, for the most part, she should be avoided. Sure, it was understood that once in a while the phantom might sneak up, unsolicited, and confide some shocking revelation, but they believed if they tried to pry the confidences out of the spirit, her troubles or mistakes could be passed on to them.

The Alice Keck Park Memorial Garden, also located in Santa Barbara, is a beautiful 4.6-acre city park. It contains seventy-five different species of plants and trees, picnic areas, hiking paths, a gazebo, and a koi pond. It also has a shadowy male ghost. Perhaps the spectre is lonely, because he's been known to follow people home and take up residence in their houses. The uninvited guest is never visible outside of the park, but his presence can be felt. The phantom isn't dangerous, but he does cause people anxiety and sleeplessness. The spirit pretty much stays as long as he wants to, but sometimes all it takes to get him to leave is to acknowledge his presence.

Los Prietos Campground is another haunted site in Greater Santa Barbara, and it's located about 14 miles north of downtown on the Santa Ynez River. It's close to the small community of Paradise in the Los Padres National Forest. The ghost of a young girl with broken arms sometimes roams the campground at night. When spotted, she's usually crying. But don't approach to console her. People who have made the mistake of speaking to her were possessed by her evil spirit and needed a priest's blessing to cast out the demon.

Haunted Trails

The Sierra Club Trail is a moderate 4.3-mile loop that encircles much of Elings Park. It has moderate foot traffic and is both kid and dog friendly. It's mountain bike friendly, too, almost to the point that in some parts of the hike it's easier to follow the bike trails than the footpaths. **Trailhead GPS: N34 24.782' / W119 44.004'**

The trail has three parts. The upper part of the path surrounds the largest section of the park, which is filled with baseball fields, tennis courts, BMX tracks, playground equipment, and picnicking spots. Two smaller paths branch off from the southern arc of the trail as it nears the intersection of Cliff Drive and Las Positas Road. The trail to the left as you face the sea is a loop walkway, and it encloses the Douglas Family Preserve. The path to the right heads down to Arroyo Burro Beach. There is a 0.4-mile out-and-back loop where the trail meets the sand.

Elings Park
1298 Las Positas Rd.
Santa Barbara, CA 93103

Alice Keck Park Memorial Garden
1500 Santa Barbara St.
Santa Barbara, CA 93101

Los Prietos Campground
111 Paradise Rd.
Santa Barbara, CA 93105

24

Cabrillo Returns

San Miguel Island, Santa Rosa Island, Santa Cruz Island
Channel Islands National Park, Santa Barbara and Ventura Counties

I N 1542 HENRY VIII executed his fifth wife, Catherine Howard; Pope Paul III established the Holy Office to oversee the Inquisition; and Mary, Queen of Scots, was born. Oh, and over in the Americas, explorer Juan Rodríguez Cabrillo discovered the Channel Islands.

Channel Islands National Park is located west of Santa Barbara and Ventura Counties. It offers protection for five islands off the shore of Southern California and the waters that immediately surround them. The entire park is one big nature preserve, so there are plenty of regulations and permits required in advance to travel to, hike, or camp on the islands.

Anacapa, the smallest island, is closest to the mainland. It's known primarily for its scenic lighthouse and Arch Rock. The next island heading westward is Santa Cruz, the largest island of the chain. Mountainous, it has one of California's famous earthquake fault lines running down its center. Santa Cruz Island has diverse flora and fauna, boasting sixty unique species. It's also the most visited of the Channel Islands. Santa Rosa, the next island to the west, is a bit smaller than Santa Cruz Island. Its hillsides are filled with rare Torrey pines, and reminders are everywhere of the sheep and cattle ranches that once peppered the isle. Furthest from the mainland is San Miguel Island. Isolated, rugged, and windswept, San Miguel has one

Scorpion Cove, Santa Cruz Island, Channel Islands National Park.
PHOTO COURTESY OF WILLIAM STRUBLE

of the world's largest breeding grounds for seals and sea lions. The island's ancient past is revealed in the trees of a caliche forest, formed eons ago when the fossilized wood became covered with salt and calcium carbonate crystals. The park's southernmost Channel Island is Santa Barbara, a high, flat mesa surrounded by rock cliffs.

(Technically, there are three more Channel Islands, but they're not part of the national park: San Nicolas, San Clemente, and Santa Catalina, the last of which has the largest resident population of all the islands. All three are located farther south than the park's five islands.)

The Channel Islands show evidence of habitation going back at least 13,000 years, but when Cabrillo arrived in 1542, the Chumash were the native peoples. Contact with the Spaniards did not go well for the Chumash. There was no armed conflict. Like elsewhere in the New World, the native tribe was decimated by European diseases for which they had no immunity. By the early nineteenth century, the Chumash had abandoned the island and moved to the mainland.

Cabrillo was on a voyage of discovery when his three ships sailed out of today's Manzanillo, Mexico, and headed up the west coast of North America. His first stop was Baja. He then anchored in San Diego and reached Catalina Island by early October. Along the way, Cabrillo claimed all of what is now California for Spain.

Soon after stopping at Catalina, he put in at Cuyler Harbor on San Miguel Island. He was unable to communicate with the locals, but he spent a week or two taking on supplies and checking out the island.

Cabrillo and his men continued up the coast. By the time they reached the mouth of the Russian River, winter was quickly approaching, and the weather was becoming harsh. Cabrillo turned south. Amazingly, he missed the entrance to San Francisco Bay in both directions, perhaps due to fog. (He was far from alone. The first recorded European discovery of the bay wasn't until 1769. And even then it was sighted by an overland expedition, not from the sea.)

For centuries it's been believed that Cabrillo returned to the safety and shelter of San Miguel Island where, soon after, he broke his shinbone, either in a fall or in a fight, possibly with natives. Whatever the cause of the injury, gangrene set in, and Cabrillo died within a week. Just before he passed, Cabrillo laid a curse on the island: Anyone who tried to live there would die by violence. The explorer was buried on the island in a lead casket.

That's the legend. But modern scholarship suggests Cabrillo sailed all the way back to Catalina Island instead of stopping at San Miguel. On his first visit to Catalina, he noted the Tongva natives were aggressive. It seems the second time around they were even less pleased to see him and his men. Around Christmas Eve, some of Cabrillo's crew got into a skirmish with the locals. Rushing to their aid, Cabrillo stumbled out of the boat as it reached the shore. He fell against a jagged rock, splintering his shin. The wound festered, and Cabrillo died of gangrene on January 3, 1543. There's no record of where he was buried, so it's possible his crew retreated to San Miguel Island and buried their captain there.

Regardless of where he was laid to rest, Cabrillo was barely in the ground before his ghost began walking the meadows of San Miguel Island. The phantom explorer is always seen wearing armor and carrying a sword with a hilt and scabbard covered with jewels.

There's another ghost on the island as well, the man that people called the "King of San Miguel Island." In 1928 World War I veteran Herb Lester had had enough of people and, through a friend, got a job as the island's caretaker. Lester subsequently leased the entire island from the US Navy to raise sheep. He lived there alone for two years in a small, one-story ranch house built by the island's former custodian. Then, while on a break to the East Coast, Lester met, fell in love with, and married Elizabeth Sherman. Together they raised two daughters on San Miguel Island, with only intermittent trips to the mainland for supplies. In 1942, in failing health, Lester took his own life with a shotgun. He was buried above Harris Point on San Miguel, and his apparition, like Cabrillo's, is now seen wandering the windblown island.

According to Dennis William Hauck, the author of *Haunted Places: The National Directory*, Santa Rosa and Santa Cruz Islands are also haunted. A weeping female spirit on Santa Rosa Island is thought to have been a sheepherder's wife who hanged herself on a weathered oak tree. Her spectre has hair down to her waist, and she wears a diaphanous gown that seems to always be fluttering in the wind—whether there's a breeze or not. She seems to float rather than walk, and she's always enveloped in an aura of soft light.

Two spooks "live" on Santa Cruz Island. One was a Chinese fisherman whose hand became pinned between two rocks while searching for abalone on the beach. No one heard his wild screams over the breaking surf as the tide started to come in. With the sea rising higher and higher and with no other recourse, he used his knife to hack off his own hand to escape. But it was to no avail. He bled to death before he could get help. His spectre now picks among the stones on the beach at Prisoners Harbor, eternally searching for his missing appendage. You'll recognize him on the beach: He'll be wearing a straw hat with a wide brim.

The other spirit on Santa Cruz Island is Mary Morrison Reese. Daniel Reese, her husband, ferried Chinese immigrants from the mainland, and it's alleged that he robbed and killed dozens, if not hundreds, of his trusting passengers over the years. Mary's ghost now roams the grounds of Christy Ranch, where she and her husband once lived.

Haunted Trails

San Miguel Island

Point Bennett Trail on San Miguel Island is a moderate, lightly trafficked, 16-mile out-and-back path that begins in Cuyler Harbor. The trail sets off to the south, then veers west to get to Point Bennett. From the lookout, you should be able to see lots of seals lounging in the sun. **Trailhead GPS: N34 02.760' / W120 21.089'**

Back in Cuyler Harbor, take time to check out the Cabrillo Monument. And if you've come to San Miguel Island to find Lester's ghost rather than for the scenery, your best bet may be to take the short, well-marked trail from the dock up to his old ranch house.

Santa Rosa Island

Ford Point Trail on Santa Rosa Island starts at the pier. This lightly trafficked trail is 19.4 miles out and back. Although it's rated as having moderate difficulty, there's an elevation gain of 1,100 feet midway through the hike, with several points having a grade of 10 to 16 percent. **Trailhead GPS: N34 00.457' / W120 02.918'**

Santa Cruz Island

Scorpion Pier is the main landing point for visitors to Santa Cruz Island. The hike from Prisoners Harbor to Chinese Harbor on Santa Cruz Island is on a difficult, lightly trafficked, 15.5-mile out-and-back trail. The hike will take 6 to 7 hours, so it's much more manageable if you're staying at Del Norte Campground overnight. From Prisoners Harbor, follow the

Navy Base Road for 1.5 miles until you reach the signposted turnoff to Del Norte Trail. From there it's 3.8 miles uphill to reach the camp. Shortly after passing the campground, the trail will split. Take the branch to the left, which leads down to the rocky beach at Chinese Harbor. As you reach the end of the trail, there's an almost hidden path to the right that leads to the shore. Make sure you bring plenty of water: You'll be climbing back up the 750-foot descent you took from the camp down to the beach. **Prisoners Harbor Trailhead GPS: N34 01.172' / W119 41.056'**

For information about visiting Channel Islands National Park, contact the National Park Service at nps.gov/chis or call (805) 658-5730.

25

The Leaper

Santa Rosa Trail, Lower Butte Trail, Wildwood Mesa Trail, Teepee Trail, Wildwood Canyon Trail, Paradise Falls
Thousand Oaks, Ventura County

MOUNT CLEF RIDGE, named for the California Lutheran Education Foundation (CLEF), is a 1,076-foot-tall volcanic bluff above Thousand Oaks in Ventura County. The ridge is overseen by the Conejo Open Space Conservation Agency, which maintains 150 miles of hiking trails over 12,400 acres.

According to legend, many hikers on the outcrop have encountered a distraught woman standing at the edge of the cliff ready to jump off. Unaware that the stranger is actually a ghost, the onlooker is horrified when the phantom looks over her shoulder, sadly and silently acknowledges the newcomer's presence, and then leaps to her "death."

If you see the apparition, whatever you do, don't walk over to the precipice. You'll suddenly be flooded with an overwhelming feeling of despair and a sudden desire to die. You'll also hear the spectre's voice echoing inside your head, urging you to jump.

If you manage to avoid taking the plunge, the woman's wraith will reappear. She'll glare at you in contempt, burrowing straight into your soul, sowing dreadful visions of death. She'll then evaporate into nothingness, leaving you to deal with your inner demons.

There's an intriguing possible source for the legend of the suicide leaper. Back in the early days of Hollywood, many silent Westerns were filmed on Mount Clef Ridge, and to excite moviegoers, replica stage-coaches and carts were sometimes deliberately pushed off the ridge and smashed on the rocks below. It's highly probable that trained stunt men and women sometimes jumped from the cliff as well during action sequences—although not suffering the same fate as the wagons. Could the troubled female phantom on Mount Clef Ridge be a revenant from the early days of Tinseltown rather than a suicide?

Whatever the origin of the ghost on Mount Clef Ridge, keep your distance from her—*and* from any nearby cliffs.

Haunted Trails

You can get a good view of Mount Clef Ridge from its base by hiking the full length of Wildwood Mesa Trail. This 2.6-mile out-and-back trail begins off Avienda de Los Arboles. It's of moderate difficulty and has fairly heavy traffic. So far there have been no reports of hikers on Wildwood Mesa Trail seeing the unhappy spectre jump off the ridge, but there's a first time for everything. **Wildwood Mesa Trailhead GPS: N34 13.185' / W118 54.144'**

While you're in the area, you may want to visit the 40-foot-tall Paradise Falls in the adjacent Wildwood Regional Park. The most direct route to the cascades is a 2.5-mile, moderately difficult out-and-back path that combines parts of Wildwood Mesa Trail and Teepee Trail. The walkway is moderately trafficked, although it's often crowded on weekends. Start at the Wildwood Mesa trailhead. Travel west for about 0.35 mile, and then left onto North Teepee Trail. After another 0.4 mile, you'll come to a T. You'll recognize the spot: It has benches, drinking water, and a replica of a teepee. **Junction GPS: N34 12.856' / W118 54.571'**

From there, turn right onto Teepee Trail. Descend for about 0.8 mile into Wildwood Canyon, and turn left when you see the sign for Paradise

Falls. A short connector path will take you to the cascades. Ducking under the falls, swimming in the pool at its base, and climbing the rocks surrounding them are prohibited.

The best path to walk along the top of the ridge is the Santa Rosa Trail, which also begins at the Wildwood Mesa trailhead. The route is rated as moderate and is heavily trafficked. Mountain bikes and dogs on a leash are allowed, and there are no permits or fees required.

Walk west on Wildwood Mesa Trail for about 0.2 mile before turning right onto Santa Rosa Trail. This main section of Santa Rosa Trail will "end" about 2.4 miles from the trailhead, where you'll see a service road to your right heading into a residential area. If you want to extend your hike on top of the ridge, stay on Santa Rosa Trail, which continues past the service road. Eventually the path will split and meet up with trails coming from farther east.

If, instead, you turn down the service road, you will hit Wildwood Avenue. Turn left at the intersection and continue down into the housing development. Just before Sundance Street, turn right onto a jogging trail that takes you all the way back to the trailhead. This final portion of the hike is Lower Butte Trail, though many consider it to be part of Wildwood Mesa Trail. Returning this way will make your hike a 4.4-mile loop.

26

The Witches' Lair

Hummingbird Trail
Simi Valley, Los Angeles County

ORNITHOLOGISTS GAVE HUMMINGBIRD TRAIL its name, but when paranormal investigators wander up this path into the hills, they're not on the lookout for birds. They're trying to locate small caves that are tucked into the canyon walls. Members of a witch coven are rumored to live in some of the grottos, and the toothless old hags have allegedly tried to abduct unsuspecting hikers.

There are numerous small caves on both sides of Hummingbird Trail, but some of them are hard to spot. In addition to these short caverns—none go in farther than a few feet—there are plenty of cracks and crevices between the boulders to explore. In at least one of the larger caves, someone has installed a sturdy swing facing the valley that allows hikers to rock away while enjoying the view below. Unfortunately, the interiors of several caves have been marred by graffiti.

Near the top of Hummingbird Trail, you'll see the Rock House, a cavern up and off to your right. (You may need to go a little way up Rocky Peak Trail to find it.) It's not a true cave, as both ends are open, yet it's not exactly a tunnel either. It's a massive boulder balanced on top of several other large rocks that create a giant, enclosed space. More than a dozen people can fit comfortably within the natural shelter.

Hiking Hummingbird Trail is an entirely different experience if you do it during a sprinkle or light rain. With cloud cover, the earthy, dark colors of the terrain really jump out. Trickles of water run down the faces of the boulders, and little pools collect in any depressions on top of the rocks. You probably don't have to worry about a flash flood rushing down Hummingbird Trail, but there may be a small stream running down the center of the path. And be extra careful of your footing when there's liquid sunshine: It doesn't take much to make the rocks slippery.

By the way, there's an upside to hiking in the rain. You probably won't be assaulted by any witches. Doesn't water make them melt?

Haunted Trails

Hummingbird Trail is a 3.7-mile out-and-back hike with an elevation gain of about 1,000 feet. Outbound, the trail makes a continuous ascent. The path's difficulty is rated hard as it winds among giant boulders and rock formations. It's a popular trail with backpackers, but it's also well-liked by mountain bikers and equestrians. Dogs are allowed on a leash. **Trailhead GPS: N34 16.819' / W118 39.716'**

The trailhead couldn't be easier to get to. Take the Kuehner Drive exit off CA 118, the Ronald Reagan Freeway. Head north toward the hills, and take your first right onto Canyon Oaks Drive. The trail starts about 750 feet on your right after you make the turn. There's usually plenty of parking, and it's free, but if nothing's available by the trailhead itself, park under the freeway bridge and take the short walk up to the path.

Unfortunately, the path is not particularly well marked. From time to time, you'll see a purple arrow on the rocks pointing you in the right direction. Pay attention if you take a side trail, because it can be difficult finding your way back to the main route. There is no shade, so take plenty of water and sunscreen. And good hiking shoes! The rocks can be very slick.

Hummingbird Trail ends when it hits Rocky Peak Trail. **Junction GPS: N34 16.522' / W118 38.315'**

If you're up for the climb, turn left at this intersection and follow the paved Rocky Peak Road up the hill as far as you like. Eventually the trail will reach Rocky Peak Park, from which there's a panoramic view of Simi Valley.

27

The Haunted Estate

Solstice Canyon Trail, Century Lake, Malibou Lake, Malibu Creek State Park
Malibu, Los Angeles County

WHEN YOU'RE IN a place like Malibu, it's hard to pull yourself away from the beach. But each year thousands of people do just that to hike nearby Solstice Canyon in the Santa Monica Mountains National Recreation Area. Most visitors enter the north–south canyon from Corral Canyon Road, which exits off Pacific Coast Highway (CA 1) about 3 miles north of Malibu.

Today, Solstice Canyon is managed by the National Park Service, but a few fascinating residences were built there before the park was created and opened to the public in 1988. Vintner and distiller "Don Mateo" Matthew Keller erected a stone cottage around 1865, and until it was destroyed in the 2007 Corral Canyon Fire, it was the oldest stone building in Malibu. Keller, an Irish immigrant, was so successful that at one point he owned 13,000 acres of Malibu and Topanga.

The home that everyone talks about, however—in part because it's said to be haunted—was built for grocer Fred Roberts and his wife, Florence. It was designed in 1952 by Paul Williams, a distinguished Southern California architect who also designed homes for such Hollywood stars as Lon Chaney, Barbara Stanwyck, Lucille Ball and Desi Arnaz, and Frank Sinatra.

Built in ranch style, the Roberts residence was spectacular—and dramatic! The home and grounds incorporated both existing and supplemental trees, local flora, streams, springs, ponds, and waterfalls. The couple named their dream house "Tropical Terrace." Fred Roberts died in 1976, but the showplace home remained, still marveling guests until it was razed by a canyon wildfire in 1982. Many hikers in Solstice Canyon take time to stop at the ruins during their treks.

People have reported feeling cold gusts of air near the old Roberts mansion and hearing ethereal, disembodied voices coming from the ruins. A few ghost hunters claim to have recorded the sounds on audiotape! (Phantom voices that are inaudible when captured and are heard for the first time upon playback are called electronic voice phenomena, or EVP.)

A few folks have also seen a dark, shadowy figure among the detritus of the mansion, and it's thought to be the spectre of Fred Roberts himself. Apparently he loved the house so much that he never left.

There's something odd going on at two lakes in the Santa Monica Mountains high above Malibu.

Century Lake, located in Malibu Creek State Park, was created around 1903 when the Crags Country Club built a 50-foot dam on its property. By the time the club closed in 1936, a 7-acre lake had been formed. 20th Century Fox purchased the land in 1946 to shoot outdoor scenes for its films and television shows.

Much of the lake has silted up, and it's now little more than a pond or marsh. Nevertheless, it supposedly has some sort of mud monster living in it. Hikers have reported seeing its grotesque head pop out of the water. One backpacker ran for his life when the creature emerged from the lake and gave chase. The hiker described the beast as being a brownish, humanoid figure with skin falling off its body like a rotting corpse. There have also been rumors that evil spirits inhabit Century Lake, so perhaps what people are seeing are ghosts, not ghouls.

Like Century Lake, Malibou Lake (with its variant spelling of Mailbu) is a man-made body of water. It's located just beyond the northwest corner of Malibu Creek State Park, very close to Agoura Hills and Thousand Oaks. The lake has also been used as a backdrop in many Hollywood movies, most famously in the scene where the Monster encounters a little girl in the original 1931 *Frankenstein*.

Malibou Lake is actually a small reservoir. It was created in 1922 by two real estate developers who bought 350 acres in the Santa Monica Mountains to build a residential lakefront community. Even though it's located where the Medea and Triunfo Creeks meet to form Malibu Creek, the lake originally took four years to fill. Like all watersheds in California, Century Lake and Malibou Lake depend on the winter rains to remain full.

The ghost of Malibou Lake is an elderly woman who swam there regularly up until her death. Known as the "Lady of the Lake," she's recognized by the swim cap she always wears. The apparition is most often spotted in the water near or standing on a small islet in the lake.

Haunted Trails

Solstice Canyon Trail

Solstice Canyon Trail is a moderate 3.2-mile, well-maintained, and heavily trafficked loop. **Trailhead GPS: N34 02.267' / W118 44.880'**

There's a parking area on Corral Canyon Road, but it's almost always crowded, often full. Once you find a place to leave your car, you may want to take advantage of the restrooms by the trailhead before you set out on your hike.

It's recommended that you follow the loop counterclockwise to get the elevation gain out of the way while you're still fresh. From the trailhead, take the set of stairs to your right. This part of the route, which heads north, is Rising Sun Trail. There's very little shade on this section of the hike, so wear sunscreen and perhaps a hat.

You'll come to an intersection known as Nest Junction about 0.7 mile into your hike (**N34 02.509' / W118 45.070'**). If you take the El Nido Trail to the left, you'll head down to the canyon floor, but stay to your right, continuing on Rising Sun Trail. Over the next mile or so you will climb another 160 feet to the highest point of your hike. As you ascend, don't forget to look to your left for views of the Pacific Ocean.

As you approach the halfway point of the hike, you'll descend though a series of switchbacks before reaching the bottom of the canyon near a stream. You'll soon see what's left of Tropical Terrace (**N34 02.965' / W118 45.11'**).

Take a well-deserved break to explore. Across the creek from the ruins, you'll see a small statue. Just east of and behind the foundations of the house is a waterfall. It's not very grand, but it's worth a peek.

Once you've taken in the remains of Tropical Terrace, head back toward the trailhead using the partly paved, partly dirt walkway. Just past the Roberts house is Sostomo Trail, which heads off to the right. If you take this 0.6-mile out-and-back side trail up the west wall of the canyon, you'll have a great panoramic view at the top. Plus, you'll see a couple of more crumbling structures along the way.

If you stay on the main trail, you'll hike about 0.8 mile before coming upon an ancient, twisted, and knotted tree. A plaque affixed to it commemorates the tree as the Keller Family Oak. The shell of Keller's stone house is visible across the river. In about 0.5 mile the path returns you to the trailhead.

Malibou Lake Trail

The hikes to Century Lake and Malibou Lake share a trailhead, and they set off from the Malibu Creek State Park parking lot. The trail to Century Lake is 3 miles out and back. The hike can be extended to 6.6 miles out and back if you want to include Malibou Lake. There's an optional trail along Century Lake on the return. **Trailhead GPS: N34 05.789' / W118 43.004'**

The hike as far as Century Lake is relatively easy, but the rest of the Malibou Lake Trail is of moderate difficulty, and both parts are heavily trafficked. On the outbound hike, stay on High Road Trail after leaving the parking area. This takes you along the north side of Century Lake, where the trail changes its name to Crags Road.

If you continue past the lake, you'll pass through a scenic area of upright volcanic rocks known as the Goat Buttes. From there it's about 0.5 mile until you come to the remains of set pieces left behind after filming ended for the television series *M*A*S*H*. Among the relics are a burned-out jeep and ambulance, and you may recognize a flattened area that served as the helicopter landing pad. In about another mile, you'll reach the southeastern tip of Malibou Lake.

On the return trip, you may want to take Forest Trail, which skirts the south shore of Century Lake. The path is both shaded and lightly trafficked. It meets Crags Road/High Road Trail at the old dam that formed Century Lake. Don't try to walk across or slide down the dam! If you injure yourself and can't run away, you might become the mud monster's next meal.

28

The Missing Children

Murphy Ranch
Pacific Palisades, Los Angeles County

MURPHY RANCH TRAIL, located in Rustic Canyon Park near Pacific Palisades, is a moderate-difficulty 3.4-mile loop with moderate traffic. It offers some lovely views of the ocean and the Santa Monica Mountains. The big draw for ghost hunters is Murphy Ranch, the haunted remains of a pro-Nazi compound from pre–World War II.

In the run-up to America entering the war, there were many Nazi sympathizers in the United States, including a strong faction in Los Angeles. A German official named Herr Schmitt convinced two converts to the cause, Winona and Norman Stephens, to fund the construction of a remote Aryan retreat to the tune of $4 million. The refuge was to be used by National Socialist Party members after fighting spread to America. Anarchy was expected until the Nazis could restore order, so the Pacific Palisades sanctuary was designed to be self-sustaining.

The US government was secretly monitoring the operation at "Murphy Ranch," of course, but no laws were being broken because America was not yet in the war. Pearl Harbor changed that. Almost immediately after the Japanese attack, federal agents moved in and arrested Schmitt and several confederates for espionage.

Murphy Ranch was completely abandoned and fell into ruin. Not much remains. A nondescript concrete building at one end of the complex once stored up to 20,000 gallons of diesel fuel, and it also housed a generator to power the ranch. It now stands derelict and graffiti-strewn. There are traces of former gardens and decaying staircases in the area as well. Farther up the road is a dilapidated two-story steel-frame building that acted as a garage and machine shed. A four-story mansion that was to be designed by architect Paul Williams—the same architect responsible for the Tropical Terrace in Solstice Canyon (see chapter 27)—was never built.

Several local children supposedly disappeared during the compound's construction, and rumor has it they were kidnapped and brainwashed or possibly became the subjects of Nazi medical experiments. Hikers in Rustic Canyon hear the youngsters' disembodied, plaintive wails and pleas. Even more disconcerting, their pale apparitions, with vacant faces and hollow, red eyes, sometimes peep out from behind trees along the park's loop trail. Backpackers who arrive around twilight are sometimes greeted by a solitary, piercing, anguished scream. No source for the sounds has ever been discovered.

Haunted Trails

The trailhead to Rustic Canyon Park and the remnants of Murphy Ranch is near the intersection of Casale Road and Capri Drive. There's no parking lot for the trail, so you'll have to find a spot on the street. **Trailhead GPS: N34 03.655' / W118 30.238'**

Walk west on Casale Road. It will become the Sullivan Ridge Fire Road as you continue uphill. After about 0.4 mile, there will be a signpost marking the Rustic Canyon entrance of Topanga State Park.

About 0.66 of a mile inside the park, you'll see a break in the chain-link fence on the left side of the fire road. Pass through it and descend a concrete staircase that seems to go on forever. There are more than 500 steps, and they'll take you down into Rustic Canyon. At the bottom of the staircase, you'll find a road to the right that goes farther into the canyon. Follow it to the abandoned Murphy Ranch.

(If you miss the hole in the fence, there's a second staircase into the canyon that's about 0.15 mile farther up the fire trail. It's near an old water tower and a disintegrating stone gate that used to be the main entrance to Murphy Ranch.)

As you walk through what's left of Murphy Ranch, you'll notice a path to the left that goes uphill. It connects with Backbone Trail in Will Rogers State Park. Don't take it. Stay on the canyon trail. When you come to the entrance of Camp Josepho, take the paved road to the right instead. This path heads up to Sullivan Ridge Fire Road and back to the trailhead where you parked.

29

The Materializing Mansion

East Ridge Trail (Inspiration Point Walking Trail), West Ridge Hiking Trail (Western High Way Trail), Runyon Canyon Fire Road Trail, Runyon Canyon Park
West Hollywood, Los Angeles County

G IVEN THE AMOUNT of open space and the relative tranquility in Runyon Canyon, it's hard to imagine that it was once "party central" for some of Hollywood's elite. It's said that from time to time, the mansion where all the festivities took place makes an appearance, even though the house was leveled long ago.

A bit of history before the ghost stories and the hiking tips begin. Runyon Canyon is located in the Santa Monica Mountains, which stretch about 40 miles from the Pacific Ocean to the Hollywood area. The relative shape of Runyon Canyon is that of a horseshoe. The curve in the "U" is the high bluff at the northern end of the canyon.

Long before Europeans arrived, Tongva Native Americans most likely inhabited the hillside cleft. By the time settlers from back East arrived, the place was nicknamed "No Man's Canyon," perhaps because of the chasm's isolation, its unsuitability for farming, or the fact that no one was living there. In 1867 the federal government gave the 167 acres within the canyon's walls to a lively character named "Greek George" Caralambo to thank him for his help with the Camel Corps—the army's short-lived experiment using camels to transport supplies from St. Louis to Los Angeles.

From 1874 to 1919, Alfredo Solano, a civil engineer, owned the property. Then Carman Runyon, a retired businessman, purchased it to have a private riding and hunting area. He renamed the gorge for himself, Runyon Canyon, and the moniker has stuck.

While in town to film a movie in 1929, Irish tenor John McCormack visited what Runyon modestly referred to as his "cabin." It was actually an elegant mansion, but the grounds were still rustic, sporting a variety of flora, including pine, sumac, and oak trees, sagebrush, toyon, and prickly pear. McCormack was so enamored of the place that he convinced Runyon to sell it to him the following year. The new owner soon added terraced gardens to the western wall of the canyon and lined the paved driveway from the gates to the house with palm trees.

Over the next decade, John Barrymore, Will Rogers, and Basil Rathbone were among the many celebrated visitors to McCormack's home. Occasionally, stars such as Janet Gaynor and Charles Boyer rented the property while McCormack was out on concert tour.

McCormack returned to Ireland for good in 1937, and five years later George Huntington Hartford II, heir to the A&P grocery chain, bought the estate. He added guesthouses, a pool, a tennis court, and other amenities. He also upgraded the mansion and gave it a new name: The Pines. Hartford was more interested in developing the property than living there, however. He proposed turning all of Runyon Canyon into a country club, but when his permit requests were denied, he tried to sell the whole kit and caboodle to the city. Unbelievably, it turned down the offer.

In 1964 Hartford sold the estate to Jules Berman, who envisioned building luxury homes in the gorge. The project was never realized, but in anticipation of city approval, Berman razed The Pines and all of the outer buildings. Then, in 1972, a wildfire swept through the canyon and destroyed anything that was still standing. In 1984 the City of Los Angeles and the

Ruins of the McCormack mansion, Runyon Canyon.
PHOTO COURTESY OF TOM OGDEN

Santa Monica Mountains Conservancy acquired the property and turned it into Runyon Canyon Park.

Hikers and joggers abound in the park, especially on the weekends, so all of the trails are heavily trafficked. The place is very pet friendly. On the lower half of the property, dogs must be kept on a leash, but in the north end of the canyon (past an inner gate) dogs are allowed to roam free, off-leash, if accompanied by their owners or walkers.

As an urban recreational area, the park draws an eclectic crowd. Immediately after you enter the gate at Fuller Avenue, there's a broad expanse of grass to the left encircled by a low, vine-covered wire fence. The field was once the massive front lawn of The Pines. In the mornings it's filled with yoga enthusiasts, and it remains a popular exercise spot throughout the day.

Just past the meadow, also on your left, are five concrete steps and parts of the old mansion's foundations, including a low, flat cement platform. You have to look carefully to see them; they've been overgrown by trees and brush and are almost completely hidden. There are also ruins of some of the outbuildings scattered around the canyon. The old tennis court is unusable and fenced off for safety.

For years, people have reported seeing a tall, slim man dressed in fashionable mid-century attire sitting on a set of concrete stairs that led up to the front door of the mansion. The seemingly solid gentleman never acknowledges the passersby, and as they watch, he silently stands, turns, and walks up the steps, only to disappear at the landing.

Some folks have heard soft music and the muted sounds of a party in full swing emanating from the empty platform behind the staircase. Others have seen colorful, twinkling orbs hovering over the foundations, about 20 to 30 feet in the air, at about the height of a second-story window. On very rare occasions, something truly astonishing takes place: The air begins to feel thicker and seems to quiver. Then, slowly, the apparition of The Pines—the residence that once stood at that very spot—materializes, looking the same way it did in the 1930s. After a few moments, the phantom mansion fades back into nothingness. Plan your day carefully if you want to see any of the phenomena. They almost always occur at dusk.

Hauntings also occur in Wattles Park, which abuts the western edge of Runyon Canyon. In addition to botanical gardens and a stream, Wattles Park contains the historic Wattles mansion, which was built in 1907.

The ghost of an elderly lady has been seen inside the former residence, especially through an upstairs window. The old woman is thought to be the original owner's first wife, who died in the house. There's also an eerie Woman in White who strolls Wattles Park at night, but it's unclear whether she's the same spirit as the one seen inside the mansion. The sound of a disembodied horse has been heard galloping in the gardens, and a woman's incorporeal screams sometimes pierce the dark.

Haunted Trails

There are three main hikes through Runyon Canyon that connect the mouth of the gorge with the north entrance on the cliff. They all pass by or overlook the ruins of The Pines. The trails are mostly even but steep, so the hike is considered to be of moderate to hard difficulty. The southern terminus for all of these hikes is the North Fuller Street Avenue entrance to the park in the City of West Hollywood. **Trailhead GPS: N34 06.317' / W118 20.940'**

By far the busiest of the park's hiking routes is the East Ridge Trail, also known as the Inspiration Point Walking Trail. To take it, pass through the Fuller Avenue gates into the canyon. At first you'll be on the paved former driveway. At about the 0.5-mile point into your walk, you'll see the connector trail to your left that leads to the park's Vista entrance. Continue straight. Before long, you'll see the mansion ruins, also on your left.

Soon you'll pass through the dog fence, after which point canines can roam unleashed. The now-dirt trail takes a hard U-turn to the right and up the hill. The path widens and immediately begins to climb sharply. The trail will take another horseshoe bend, and the angle of ascent will increase. At the 0.45-mile mark, you'll reach the large, flat viewing area known as Inspiration Point. This is a perfect place to pause to admire the view. On a clear day you can see as far as downtown Los Angeles and the Pacific Ocean.

Continue up the trail, which quickly becomes narrower and steeper. At the 0.8-mile point of the hike, you'll reach Clouds Rest, which, as its name suggests, is a great place to stop to catch your breath. The view is as spectacular as it was at Inspiration Point, perhaps even more so. At 0.95 mile, you'll see a turnoff to the left. This is the Runyon Canyon Fire Road, and it heads back down to the canyon floor. If you take it, you reach the Vista Street gate. From there, turn left onto the connector trail that leads to the mansion's old driveway. Turn right to return to the Fuller Avenue entrance, having made a 1.9-mile loop.

If you want to hike both ridges of the canyon, don't turn left onto Runyon Canyon Fire Road after passing Clouds Rest. At the split, continue straight (or bear slightly right) up the path. At this point, the trail merges into the northern extension of the Runyon Canyon Fire Road. Four-tenths of a mile farther, turn left onto the Western High Way Trail, also known as the West Ridge Hiking Trail. In just 0.3 mile you will approach the western edge of the park. Turn left down the ridge. (If you reach Solar Drive, you've gone too far.) Continue hiking down this western "wall" of the canyon until it meets the lower section of Runyon Canyon Fire Road. Follow the fire road to the Visa Street gate, then take the connector trail that leads to the driveway and the Fuller Avenue entrance. This loop is 2.65 miles long.

It's also possible to continue all the way to the park's northern Mulholland Drive entrance during your hike. From the Fuller gate, follow the East Ridge Trail through Inspiration Point and Clouds Rest. Pass Western High Way Trail, and continue walking the upper portion of Runyon Canyon Fire Road all the way to Mulholland Drive. If you reach Mulholland you will actually be outside the canyon, so just before you do, bear left onto a very obvious separate trail that keeps you inside the canyon. Almost immediately there will be a short connector path on your right. Take it if you want to visit an overlook at the highest point of the park.

Otherwise, continue straight. This path will soon intersect the Western High Way Trail, and you know what to do from there: Turn right onto the trail and then left just before reaching Solar Drive. Descend the ridge. Take Runyon Canyon Fire Road to the Vista gate, and then cut back to the Fuller Avenue entrance. This loop is 3.3 miles long.

Taking the Western High Way/West Ridge Trails affords an extra opportunity: They pass closest to Wattles Mansion.

Runyon Canyon Park is open to the public seven days a week from dawn to dusk. In addition to the Fuller Avenue entrance, the Runyon Canyon Vista entrance offers a second way into the southern end of the park. It's located about 0.2 mile west of Fuller. The north entrance to the canyon, high up on the ridge, is accessed from Mulholland Drive, a winding road that follows the crest of the Santa Monica Mountains. This upper entrance to the canyon is at the intersection of Pyramid Place and Mulholland Drive. **Trailhead GPS: N34 07.188' / W118 21.183'**

Parking at both the base of the canyon and along Mulholland Drive is extremely limited. If you do find an empty space, make sure to check the parking restrictions before leaving your car.

Obviously, it's possible to hike either way on the trails, up or down the canyon ridges, and it's possible to combine two or more trails to form a loop. Whichever route you take through Runyon Canyon Park, the hike is sure to be invigorating. Especially if you run into one of the ghosts.

30

Hollywoodland

**Mount Lee Drive Trail, Wonder View Trail, Hollyridge Trail,
Canyon Drive Trail**
Hollywood, Los Angeles County

WHEN A STRUGGLING actress kills herself by jumping off the "H" in the HOLLYWOOD sign on Mount Lee overlooking La La Land, it's more than just a suicide: It's a statement! The problem is, when one ingénue did, nobody was sure what the message was that she wanted to convey. Perhaps that's why her ghost is still seen on the trails leading up to the sign—and on the sign itself.

Nicknamed Peg, Millicent Lilian Entwistle was born in Wales in 1908. She moved to America with her father while she was still a young child. After her father's death, Peg was adopted by her Uncle Charles and Aunt Jane. She soon became involved in the Boston theater scene, then made her official debut on Broadway in 1926. Over the next six years she appeared in ten Broadway productions.

In 1932 producers brought Peg Entwistle to Los Angeles to be in a new play, *The Mad Hopes*, starring Billie Burke and Humphrey Bogart. She moved into her uncle's new house on North Beachwood Drive, located beneath the HOLLYWOOD sign—except that at the time, the nine-year-old sign actually read HOLLYWOODLAND. It was an advertising billboard for a Hollywood Hills real estate development.

Scouts from Radio Pictures (later known as RKO) spotted the attractive young blonde, blue-eyed actress in *The Mad Hopes* and scheduled a screen test. She was given a one-film contract with the studio's option to extend.

The movie was *Thirteen Women*, starring Irene Dunne and Myrna Loy. Entwistle only had a minor role in the large ensemble, but when the movie was edited she was all but cut from the film. Then, when the studio declined to offer her a new contract, Peg was devastated.

On September 16, 1932, 24-year-old Peg Entwistle followed one of the old paths up to the HOLLYWOODLAND sign, climbed to the top of the 50-foot-tall, 30-foot-wide "H," and jumped off.

Two days later, a hiker discovered Entwistle's lifeless body in the ravine far below the sign. It was two more days before Peg's uncle and aunt realized that their missing niece might be the person the newspapers were calling "the Hollywood Sign Girl."

Was Entwistle so distraught by her initial failure that she decided she had lost her only chance to become a movie star? Was her desire to "make it" in the City of Broken Dreams so strong that she refused to return to New York and pick up her theater career? Or was there some other struggle going on in her personal life that has never come to light?

Perhaps we'll never know for certain. Even her suicide note, which was found in her purse at the base of the sign, gave little insight into her decision. It read simply: "I'm afraid I'm a coward. I am sorry for everything. If I had done this thing a long time ago it would have saved a lot of pain. P.E."

As it turned out, Peg's career would have been far from over. A day or two after she died, a letter from the Beverly Hills Playhouse arrived at her uncle's house offering Entwistle the lead role in a new drama. Ironically, at the end of the play, her character committed suicide.

Peg's body was cremated and her ashes were interred in her father's grave back in Glendale, Ohio. But her spirit hasn't stayed there. It's returned to haunt the trails leading up to and around the HOLLYWOOD sign as well as the towering "H" itself.

She doesn't appear often, but people still report seeing the spectre of a young woman struggling her way up through the scrub to the base of the HOLLYWOOD sign. Frequently when the spirit appears, onlookers smell gardenias, the scent of Peg's favorite perfume—even when the flowers aren't in bloom. Occasionally, folks spy Entwistle's ghost standing on the top of the enormous "H." Believing the phantom was flesh and blood, people have called the police to come rescue the woman. Now and then, Peg's apparition is even spotted walking north on Beachwood Drive, heading toward the sign.

Trying to get close to the sign has never been easy, even in Peg Entwistle's time. Mount Lee is within the public, city-owned Griffith Park, but the sign was never designed to be a tourist attraction, so it wasn't made accessible. At the time, who would have wanted to hike up a steep cliff just to touch a billboard? It wasn't until after the Hollywood Chamber of Commerce acquired the sign in 1949 and removed the last four letters that it became a true landmark. It's now iconic, the very symbol of Tinseltown.

Unfortunately, because of vandalism and accidents in the past, you're no longer allowed to walk up to the front of the sign. In 2000 the Los Angeles Police Department installed motion detectors and closed-circuit cameras to prevent anyone from getting within 50 yards of the letters. But you can still get pretty darn close.

Haunted Trails

Fortunately, there are several trails on Mount Lee that will take you to a small plateau above and behind the sign. From there you can see the backs of the letters and a panorama of the city. **Overlook GPS: N34 08.074' / W118 19.316'**

Many backpackers used to park in the cul-de-sac at the northern end of Deronda Drive to start their hike. From there they would pass around a gate and follow Mount Lee Drive, a paved fire road, to the top of Mount Lee. Recently, though, the city has restricted nonresident parking due to the sheer volume of tourist traffic that was clogging the very narrow, winding road. It's not currently against the law to walk the Mount Lee fire trail. You just can't park anywhere near the Deronda Drive cul-de-sac. **Gate GPS: N34 07.810' / W118 19.154'**

Brush Canyon Trail, also known as Canyon Drive Trail, begins at the north end of Canyon Drive near Camp Hollywood in Bronson Canyon. It's a 6.1-mile out-and-back hike of moderate difficulty. Brush Canyon Trail heads uphill and will "T" at Mulholland Trail. (This is actually the Mulholland Fire Trail, which starts on the east side of Griffith Park.) Turn left onto Mulholland Trail. After many curves, the path will pass the Hollywoodridge Trail (more about that later) and "T" at Mount Lee Drive. Turn right and continue to the HOLLYWOOD sign. **Brush Canyon Trailhead GPS: N34 07.397' / W118 18.908'**

Fun fact. If you hike Brush Canyon Trail, there's a side trip worth considering. Just before you reach Camp Hollywood on Canyon Drive, there's a paved street to the right. The road is blocked to vehicular traffic and almost immediately turns to dirt. If you walk around the gate and follow the path for about 2,500 feet, you'll reach Bronson Caves. They're not caves at all but short tunnels that were dug as part of an old rock quarry. You may recognize the mouth of the East Portal because it served as the entrance to the Batcave in the 1966–1968 *Batman* television series starring Adam West and Burt Ward. You just hummed the theme song, didn't you? **Bronson Caves Trailhead GPS: N34 07.467' / W118 18.857'**

The 3.5-mile round-trip Hollywoodridge Trail is one of the shortest hikes to the HOLLYWOOD sign. The ascent is only about 750 feet in elevation. The trail begins close to the equestrian stables at Sunset Ranch Hollywood, which is located at the northern end of North Beachwood Drive. The trailhead is on the right side of Beachwood before you reach the ranch. Unfortunately, the ranch complained that the number of hikers interfered with its operations, so the city closed the trail in 2017. If the pathway ever reopens, you'll be able to hike uphill from the trailhead, and in about 1,000 feet, the path will "T" at Mulholland Trail. Turn left onto

Mulholland. After several bends, the path will "T" at Mount Lee Drive. Turn right and follow the ridge to the HOLLYWOOD sign. **Trailhead GPS: N34 07.763' / W118 18.886'**

Wonder View Trail (also known as the Tree of Life Trail) begins on the northwest side of the Santa Monica Mountains. The hike is about 3.7 miles out and back. Traffic is moderate, but the difficulty is hard. You will gain an elevation of 1,368 feet on this route. To get to the trailhead, take Lake Hollywood Drive from Barham Boulevard. At a bend in the road, you'll reach the intersection of Lake Hollywood Drive and Wonder View Drive. The upper section of Wonder View Drive has no side-of-road parking, and turning around is difficult, so don't even drive up there. Park somewhere in the immediate area, but be careful to check signage for restrictions. Walk up Wonder View Drive. You'll see a sign saying there is no access to the HOLLYWOOD sign, but that's for cars, not hikers. Foot traffic is not a problem. **Trailhead GPS: N34 08.083' / W118 20.078'**

About a third of the way to the HOLLYWOOD sign, you'll reach a lesser-known landmark, the Wisdom Tree. It will be another very demanding 1 or 2 miles until you get to the HOLLYWOOD sign. **Wisdom Tree GPS: N34 08.161' / W118 19.925'**

Keep in mind that although all of these trails are fairly even, they're all very steep. There are no toilet facilities. And there is no shade and no water fountains, so bring plenty of sunscreen (even on cloudy days) and lots of water—but as experienced hikers, you already know that.

For those who just want to take selfies and group shots with a close, unobstructed view of the sign, there's a sanctioned parking area in Lake Hollywood Park that gives you a perfect angle. From the viewpoint, visitors can even make out the faint, untended old path that wends its way from the ravine, up through the undergrowth on the hillside, to the bottom of the sign's massive "D." The track falls apart before it reaches the letter, however, and a large crevice has been eroded into the unstable, sandy soil. Little wonder the pathway is off-limits. **Viewpoint GPS: N34 07.427' / W118 19.543'**

31

The Ghosts of Griffith Park

Old Zoo Trail, Bee Rock Trail, Haunted Picnic Table 29, Griffith Park, Corralitas Red Car Trail
Los Angeles, Los Angeles County

LOCATED IN LOS Angeles at the eastern end of the Santa Monica Mountains, Griffith Park is a 4,300-acre urban recreational area. There are dozens of marked and unmarked trails on the terrain, much of it mountainous, so paths vary from moderate to hard difficulty.

As for its ghosts, well, the story starts more than 200 years ago.

Spaniards first visited the region in 1769. Twelve years later, José Vicente Feliz, acting as a military escort, accompanied eleven Mexican families to Alta California, where they founded the pueblo of Los Angeles. From 1787 to about 1800, Feliz served as the town's manager, effectively making him the sheriff and judge, as well as liaison with the local Tongva-Gabrieleno tribes. Upon Feliz's retirement, the Spanish Crown gifted him 6,647 acres that stretched north along the Los Angeles River from what is now downtown L.A.

In due course, Don José Antonio Feliz, the brother-in-law of the widow of one of Vicente's sons—did you follow that?—became owner of the property. He remained a bachelor, but his sister, Soledad, and an orphaned niece, Doña Petranilla, lived with him.

Antonio Feliz contracted smallpox in 1860, which proved to be fatal. When he was on his deathbed, a prosperous rancher and merchant named Don Antonio Coronel showed up with a lawyer, Don Innocante, to "help" Feliz prepare a will. Unsurprisingly, Coronel wound up inheriting Feliz's ranch. Soledad got some furniture. Petranilla had married, and her son received a few horses, but Petranilla herself got nothing. Nothing! The family heirs disputed the will, of course—it was never witnessed or signed—and the case made it as far as the California Supreme Court. But with proverbial "friends in high places," Coronel prevailed. Enraged, Petranilla laid a curse on Don Coronel, Innocante, the presiding judge, everyone who would ever own the property, and the land itself.

So how did the curse work out? The lawyer was shot and killed during an argument. The judge died an early death. The river flooded the ranch in the winter, there were droughts in the summer, and there were constant wildfires in between. After his cattle died and the crops failed, Coronel was forced to sell the property. Much of the former Feliz ranch was eventually purchased by Col. Griffith Jenkins Griffith. A Welshman, Griffith had come to America in 1865 and became a multimillionaire speculating in gold mines.

Griffith opened an ostrich farm on the land, but it never took off. His attempt to subdivide the property into small parcels didn't work out either. In 1896 Griffith surprised everyone by giving 3,015 acres of the ranch—about 5 square miles—to the City of Los Angeles. His only stipulation was that it "be made a place of recreation and rest for the masses, a resort for the rank and file, for the plain people."

Though suspicious of his motives, the city accepted the offer. Griffith was not a popular man, so most people decided he did it for the good will. Detractors suggested he needed a tax break. Still others suspected that Griffith had begun to believe the curse was real—or had actually been visited by the ghost of Doña Petranilla.

Whatever the reason, Griffith's misfortunes continued. And on top of everything, he seemed to be slowly going insane. He became convinced that his Catholic wife, Christina, was trying to poison him on orders from the pope! In 1903, in an alcoholic rage, he shot Christina. She survived, but Griffith was found guilty of attempted murder and spent a year in San Quentin. After his release, he lived another fifteen years, but he was a social outcast. He died of liver failure, a broken man, in 1919.

For some reason, Griffith willed the rest of his property to the city for a public park with the caveat that it would be named for him. He also left $700,000 to build an observatory and a theater.

A century later, Griffith Park is home to the HOLLYWOOD sign, the Griffith Observatory, the Greek Theatre, a merry-go-round, a railroad museum, a transportation museum, a zoo, biological gardens, the Autry Museum of the American West, a golf course—and at least four ghosts.

One of them is the restless Doña Petranilla. Her spectre has been appearing since at least 1884, when her ghostly figure materialized during a thunderstorm. She's always dressed in white, and she's been spotted on pathways throughout the park and inside the original Feliz adobe that's now part of the ranger station.

After Coronel died in 1894, his apparition began to be seen late at night in the northeastern section of the park, where the zoo and golf course are located. He's also been observed on the high trails. His harrowing cry—more of a howl, really—occasionally echoes down from the hills. And on clear nights his dark outline has been seen on top of a formation known as Bee Rock, silhouetted against the moon. Sometimes his ghost is on foot, sometimes on horseback.

A different phantom horseback rider has been seen galloping over the property. Many suppose the wraith in the saddle is Doña Petranilla. Others are certain it's Griffith J. Griffith.

The 133-acre Los Angeles Zoo and Botanical Gardens opened in Griffith Park in 1966. The zoological garden is known for its Campo Gorilla Reserve, its Chimpanzees of the Mahale Mountains exhibit, and the Red Ape Rain Forest. The facility replaced the old Griffith Park Zoo, which had welcomed guests from 1912 to mid-1966.

Old Zoo Trail, Griffith Park.
PHOTO COURTESY OF MARK WILLOUGHBY

Even though the old zoo's animals are long gone, many of the cages and rock enclosures remain, standing empty and abandoned. Rather than remove them, the city decided to keep some of the historic cages and walkways in place because, as a park sign notes, they are "home to memories of family visits to the Griffith Park Zoo, as well as an opportunity to better understand developments in the zoological sciences."

The animals themselves were relocated, but psychics have claimed to sense revenants of some of the creatures still languishing in the old zoo. Some sort of spirit residual must remain: Visitors to the grounds have heard roars, trumpets, growls, and the general clatter of caged animals. And the current zoo is more than 2 miles away, so the sounds aren't drifting over from there.

If that's not enough ghost stories for you, Griffith Park also has a haunted picnic table! The story goes that on Halloween night 1976, a starry-eyed couple took a romantic walk up Mt. Hollywood Drive, which starts in the northeast corner of the park. Along the way, they sat down to rest at a picnic table. Without warning, an overhanging tree branch snapped off and fell directly on top of the young lovers, killing them both. After their funerals, their families decided to spread the couple's ashes at the site.

Oh, and about that branch. It's said that a tree trimmer was sent out to remove it, but once there, he soon became uncomfortable. It was as if some strange, evil aura surrounded the table, and he fled. When he got back to his truck, the words "next you die" were scrawled on his windshield. Another man was sent out to take care of the job. His dead body, with no evidence of foul play, was later found slumped on the ground near the table and broken limb. He had died of a heart attack. He couldn't call for help because his radio was mysteriously malfunctioning. In the end, no other maintenance worker would agree to touch the tree limb, so it's still there, lying across the table.

The table—Picnic Table 29—has become somewhat of a paranormal destination. In fact, ghost hunters often leave behind small, occult-themed tokens of respect. Visitors sometimes feel a sudden dip in temperature and hear the couple's disembodied moans. Phones and other electronic equipment have broken or failed at the location as well. Many people have reported getting chest pains or feeling that they were being smothered while standing near the infamous table. Still others claimed to have found the "next you die" warning scribbled on their own windshields—or, in one case, scratched into the person's flesh.

Doña Petranilla's curse seems to have been lifted for now, because there have been fewer reports of supernatural sightings in recent years. Griffith Park is safe, but it *is* an urban wilderness. Besides other hikers and mountain bikers, you'll be sharing the place with coyotes, mountain lions, and snakes. Be aware of your surroundings. Griffith Park doesn't need another ghost.

Less than 5 miles from Griffith Park, it's possible to walk a haunted trail that was once part of the historical Red Car trolley system that stretched across Greater Los Angeles during the first half of the twentieth century. After World War II, with an abundance of new highways being built and cars becoming affordable for the middle class, automobiles replaced trolleys as the preferred method of transportation.

As the Red Cars went out of business, most of their tracks, bridges, and overhead wires were torn up for scrap. What remained behind were the strips of land that ran under viaducts or served as rail beds. One of the few stretches that has managed to remain undeveloped is now a suburban walkway, the Corralitas Red Car Trail, also known as the Corralitas Rail Path. From 1906 to 1955 it was part of the Pacific Electric Railway Company's trolley route between Glendale and downtown.

The trail can be accessed from either end, and there is usually street parking. The landscape varies from open fields to a shaded canyon. Dogs on leashes are allowed. During your walk, you'll see the remnants of some concrete footings that once supported trestles and passenger platforms. These foundation blocks were named an L.A. Historic-Cultural Monument in 2003.

It's long been rumored that the dirt trail is haunted. The apparitions tend to materialize around twilight. They're believed to be the unhappy spirits of anonymous laborers who died during construction of the trolley line and were buried alongside or under the track.

Haunted Trails

Old Zoo Trail

It's perfectly permissible to stroll through the old zoo. After passing the last few cages, the paved walkway ends. Three dirt paths set out from this general area. The first two, the Lower Old Zoo Trail and the Upper Old Zoo Trail, turn south and slope upward behind the decaying enclosures. The upper trail is, naturally, at a higher elevation. The far ends of both trails intersect Fern Canyon Trail. As a result, it would be an easy matter to combine the two Old Zoo Trails into a loop. **Lower Old Zoo Trailhead GPS: N34 08.099' / W118 17.404'; Upper Old Zoo Trailhead GPS: N34 08.108' / W118 17.418'**

Bee Rock, Griffith Park.
PHOTO COURTESY OF CHRISTINE COX

Bee Rock

Bee Rock is a layered, domed stone formation in the shape of an upside-down hornet's nest. The path to its top shares the trailhead for the Upper Old Zoo Trail. **Trailhead GPS: N34 08.108' / W118 17.418'**

To hike Bee Hive Trail, go straight uphill rather than turning left behind the old zoo cages. The winding path to the top is very steep and a real workout, taking you to an elevation of 1,056 feet. At the end, however, you're rewarded with a grand view of the entire east side of Griffith Park. The summit of Bee Rock is enclosed by guardrails to prevent falls. **Summit GPS: N34 08.064' / W118 17.624'**

Table 29

It's unknown which route the tragic couple followed to get to Table 29, but one of the shortest ways to get there is to park at the Mineral Wells Picnic Area on Griffith Park Drive and hike up North Trail. From the trailhead, a short connector path immediately hits Mineral Wells Trail. Jog right onto North Trail and head uphill. The trail will pass Amir's Garden, an ornamental rest area, and eventually intersect a paved road, Vista Del Valle Drive. Turn right. Follow Vista Del Valle Drive until it "T"s at Mt. Hollywood Drive, which is also paved. Take Mt. Hollywood a short way downhill. Table 29 will be clearly visible on the left side of the road. **North Trailhead GPS: N34 08.700' / W118 17.625'**

Another "trail" to the picnic table is worth mentioning, because it's impossible to get lost along the way. The problem is that it climbs steadily and is much, much longer than other routes. The path starts out on a paved but unnamed fire road closed to traffic, but it becomes Mt. Hollywood Drive as you head uphill. It's okay to walk around the gated trailhead on Griffith Park Drive. Just don't drive your car to the top, even if the gate is open or unlocked. The road is for park vehicles only. A few yards before you reach Vista Del Valle Drive, Table 29 will be on the right side of the road. **Trailhead GPS: N34 08.996' / W118 17.997'**

There's a possible bonus to this second route if you're an avid moviegoer. About 0.3 mile before you reach the picnic table there's a hairpin turn on Mt. Hollywood Drive. The bend is known as Cathy's Corner, and a major scene from the film *La La Land* was shot there. **Cathy's Corner GPS: N34 08.359' / W118 18.491'**

Corralitas Rail Trail

The Corralitas Rail Trail is about a mile long and is an easy hike. It's located in the Silverlake district south of Griffith Park near the junction of the Glendale Freeway (CA 2) and I-5. The unmarked northern entrance is on the south side of Fletcher Drive, close to the intersection of Fletcher and Riverside Drives. **North Trailhead GPS: N34 06.333' / W118 15.419'**

The south entrance of the Corralitas Rail Trail, also unmarked, is at the cul-de-sac end of Corralitas Drive. **South Trailhead GPS: N34 05.871' / W118 15.195'**

32

The Hungry, Hungry Ghosts

Mount Wilson Toll Road, Eaton Canyon Trail, Eaton Canyon Falls
Pasadena, Los Angeles County

ATON CANYON IS located in the Angeles National Forest, north of Pasadena in the foothills of the San Gabriel Mountains. Eaton Canyon Natural Area Park takes up 190 acres of the lower canyon and sits on land that was once owned by the Southern Pacific Railroad. The property is managed by the Los Angeles County Department of Parks and Recreation. The Eaton Canyon Nature Center, found within the park, has exhibits on local flora and fauna.

One of the major draws for hikers in the canyon is the old Mount Wilson Toll Road, which was begun in 1891 and operated, on and off, until 1936. It runs from Altadena to the summit of Mount Wilson, which has had a telescope or observatory on its summit since 1889.

At first the roadway could only accommodate pack animals and those on foot or horseback. The road was widened in 1907 for automobiles, but the path was still very narrow, and it was filled with sharp turns and steep drops. After the safer Angeles Crest Highway opened in 1935, there was no longer a need for the toll road, and it closed a year later. The land, including a bridge spanning Eaton Canyon, was turned over to the USDA Forest Service.

If you hike Eaton Canyon Trail and continue under the bridge instead of heading up to Mount Wilson, you'll eventually reach 50-foot Eaton

Canyon Falls, itself a popular destination. Water from the cascade forms a small but pretty pool at its base.

Feel free to stand underneath the cascade and enjoy a dip in the water. But it may be the last thing you ever do! Legend has it that malevolent apparitions—pallid skeleton-like figures with open jaws—lurk behind the waterfall awaiting a victim. Given the opportunity, they'll heinously shriek, jump out, and bite into you. They're hungry all right, but not for your flesh. Rather, you'll feel your soul being slowly drained from your body. Gather your wits about you, pull free, and run! Hikers have survived the ordeal, so it *is* possible to escape.

There are more cascades above Eaton Canyon Falls, but back in 1979 authorities shut the tunnel that led to them over safety concerns. They also stopped maintenance on the upper trail. At least three determined hikers have died trying to navigate around the blockage. The upper trail was completely closed and made off-limits by the USDA Forest Service in 2014, and those who ignore the new rules face fines and jail time.

Haunted Trails

The trail up to Mount Wilson is open to hikers, and it can be accessed via a gate on Pinecrest Drive in Altadena. This is a difficult, heavily trafficked 16.9-mile out-and-back hike, but you really can't get lost. The trail is obvious and will take you all the way up to Mount Wilson Observatory. **Trailhead GPS: N34 11.494' / W118 06.334'**

You can also reach Mount Wilson by way of the Eaton Canyon trailhead behind the Eaton Canyon Nature Center. The trail will intersect the old toll road at the bridge. If you take the path up to the road and turn right, you'll be on your way up to the observatory. Turning left will take you to Pinecrest Drive gate. **Trailhead GPS: N34 10.687' / W118 05.798'**

There's also a "shortcut" from Eaton Canyon Trail to the former toll road by way of the Walnut Canyon Trail. The turnoff from Eaton Canyon Trail is on your right. It's a very steep, twisting path, though, so you'll have to decide for yourself whether the distance you'd save would be worth the effort. **Trailhead GPS: N34 11.313' / W118 06.000'**

The hike from the nature center all the way to Eaton Canyon Falls is about 3.5 miles. It's heavily trafficked and is of moderate difficulty. On the way you'll cross over a rocky wash which, depending upon the time of year, could be completely dry or a full stream. After you've passed under the bridge, the terrain will become rougher, the trail will narrow and become rockier, and you'll have to cross the creek several times. The trail also becomes less carefully marked, but if you follow the stream you know you're heading toward the falls.

Just before reaching the cascades, ignore an unmarked, indistinct trail that cuts off to the left. The path climbs up the west side of the canyon to the top of the waterfall but is very dangerous and should be avoided. Even seasoned off-trackers and rock climbers have been injured or killed trying to follow the hazardous trail. **Base of Eaton Canyon Falls GPS: N34 11.803' / W118 06.145'**

Information for the Angeles National Forest is available by phone, Monday through Friday, at (626) 574-1613.

33

The Haunted Forest

The Cobb Estate, Sam Merrill Trail to Echo Mountain, Sunset Ridge Trail, Millard Canyon Falls Trail, Altadena Gravity Hill
Altadena, Los Angeles County

THE WOODS ABOVE the former Cobb Estate in Altadena are filled with ghosts—so much so that they've been nicknamed the Haunted Forest for more than a century!

In 1918 retired lumber magnate Charles H. Cobb built a Spanish-style mansion for his family on 107 acres in Altadena, just north of Pasadena. Cobb died in 1939. A Freemason, he willed the property to the Pasadena Scottish Rite, which in turn sold it to the Sisters of St. Joseph for use as a spiritual retreat. During all this time, there were no reports of paranormal activity taking place inside the house.

No, the stories of strange lights streaming out of the windows and weird noises echoing from inside the mansion didn't start until the Marx Brothers bought the place as an investment in 1956. The hijinks didn't come from them: They never lived there. Most likely the "phenomena" were caused by some of the 175 juveniles and 20 adults who were arrested for trespassing on the property, but who knows? Officially, the place was unoccupied.

The mansion fell into such disrepair that it was torn down in 1959, and the empty land just sat there, waiting for its next incarnation. The idea was floated of turning the acreage into a cemetery, but naturally that was met with immense opposition by the neighbors. They already had a Haunted Forest! In 1971, with the assistance of the Altadena High School Conservation Club and a generous donation from Mrs. Virginia Steele Scott, enough money was raised for the City of Altadena to buy the property and make it a public recreational area. Today, the former Cobb Estate is part of the Angeles National Forest and is administered by the USDA Forest Service.

But the rumors about ghosts persist.

The apparition of one particular person, Crystal Calhoon, along with her little dog, is said to haunt the trails on this section of the woods. Nothing is known of Calhoon's background or why it's believed she's the spectre, but she's been given two sobriquets: the Wicked Witch of the West and the Witch of Cobb Mountain. Oddly, when she's spotted, she seems to be going through the motions of vacuuming, even though she's outdoors. There's no need to panic if you see her, but people who have encountered her discover later that some possession they were carrying has gone missing. The lost or misplaced item is always a shiny object.

It's said that hikers sometimes hear disembodied screams and foot-steps in the forest, and they see bizarre lights in the distance. People have reported dark human shapes lurking on the trails, sometimes hanging from trees. (There are unsubstantiated rumors that lynchings used to take place in these woods.) Some folks have had the sensation of being fol-lowed by an invisible presence. There have even been claims of blackened stains—perhaps dried blood—on the forest floor.

Hikers on the Sunset Ridge Trail in Millard Canyon have felt inexpli-cable fear and nausea. Some folks believe that a portal to the Other World either exists or sometimes opens on the path. Those who have seen the mysterious gateway have described it as being a continuous flicker of light. Anyone who approaches it is hit by an icy burst of cold air.

Another popular hike in the Haunted Forest—although it has no ghost story attached to it—is the one to Echo Mountain. At the top of the hill you'll find the ruins of Echo Mountain House, a hotel built by

Mount Lowe Railway Trail between Echo Mountain and Sunset Point,
Angeles National Forest.
PHOTO COURTESY OF CHRISTINE COX

Thaddeus Lowe in 1894. After only six years in operation, the place caught
fire and burned to the ground. One of the few relics still standing at the
site is the "Echo Phone," a mounted metal megaphone. If you yell into it,
you'll hear why the place is called Echo Mountain.

By 1915 all of the other facilities that had been built on Echo Mountain, including three other hotels, had been destroyed by floods, wildfire, or
other natural disasters. The public soon lost all interest in Echo Mountain
as a recreational getaway.

In 1938 a deluge washed out most of the trail up Echo Mountain,
and what remained of a railway that once climbed the hillside was sold for
scrap soon after. That's where Sam Merrill comes into the story. Although
he was clerk of the Superior Court of Los Angeles, Merrill was also an
avid outdoorsman and was active with the Sierra Club. As a young man,

he even spent a summer hiking with John Muir! Merrill believed that the view from Echo Mountain, including Sunset Point at the hotel ruins, was so spectacular that the walking path to the top had to be reopened and maintained. Throughout the 1940s he personally oversaw its restoration and upkeep, and after his death in 1948, the Sierra Club named the trail in his honor.

While you're in the area, you may want to visit the haunted Altadena Gravity Hill. It's one of many stretches of highway around the country where the driver can put a car into neutral at the bottom of a hill, and the vehicle will seemingly roll uphill.

The most common ghost story associated with gravity hills is that the car is being pushed to safety by the spirits of people who died from a collision at that location. A darker version of the tale says that the angry dead are pulling the car up to the accident site so the occupants will share the phantoms' fate. Also, it's said that if you sprinkle talcum powder on your vehicle's trunk or hood before you put your car in neutral at the "bottom" of the hill, you'll see the phantoms' handprints in the powder after you've reached the top.

Spoiler alert: A gravity hill is an optical illusion created by the surrounding landscape. The vehicle is actually rolling downhill. As for the palm prints, the talc simply reveals unseen handprints of people who had previously touched the car.

Haunted Trails

Sunset Ridge Trail

Sunset Ridge Trail is a moderate, 4.4-mile out-and-back hike. The path is very popular and can be heavily trafficked. The path is partially paved, and dogs on leashes are allowed. There are also plenty of mountain bikers. Be prepared for an elevation gain of 1,198 feet from the trailhead to the turn-around point of the walk. **Trailhead GPS: N34 12.887' / W118 08.861'**

Millard Falls, Angeles National Forest.
PHOTO COURTESY OF CHRISTINE COX

There's a parking lot for the trail at the intersection of Chaney Trail Road and Mount Lowe Road, but it requires a National Forest Adventure Pass, which is not sold on-site. There's also limited street parking, but hours are very restricted. Check the signage carefully so you don't come back to find a ticket on your windshield.

The trailhead is signposted on the north side of Mount Lowe Road about 0.3 mile east of the parking lot. There will be many switchbacks on the path as it winds through and above Millard Canyon, and at one point there will be a good view of Millard Falls down to your left. If you continue on Sunset Ridge Trail after passing the falls, the path will reconnect with Mount Lowe Road. **Junction GPS: N34 13.060' / W118' 07.616'**

For all intents and purposes this is the end of the outbound hike. You can return the way you came, or you can walk downhill on Mount Lowe Road until you reach the parking lot. This paved route is not very scenic, but it's easy on the feet. Beware of mountain bikes speeding up from behind you on the roadway.

Many hikers have no doubt made their way from Sunset Ridge Trail down into the canyon to get to Millard Falls, but there's a more direct path from the Millard Campground. Parking for the campsite is the lot at the junction of Chaney Trail Road and Mount Lowe Road. Millard Canyon Falls Trail starts out from the campground. The singletrack path is narrow, and you'll cross the small creek several times as you follow it up to the falls. There's also some minor negotiating over slippery rocks. Many parts of the trail are shaded, and dogs are allowed. **Trailhead GPS: N34 12.889' / W118 08.870'**

Sam Merrill Trail

Sam Merrill Trail is a moderate-difficulty, heavily trafficked 5.4 miles out and back. The trailhead is near the intersection of East Loma Alta Drive and Lake Avenue. There's minimal street parking near the trailhead, and hours are closely regulated. **Trailhead GPS: N34 12.239' / W118 07.834'**

Start your hike by going through the gates to the Cobb Estate and follow the old driveway toward where the mansion once stood. At the first bend in the road, you'll see a sign saying "TRAIL" pointing to the right. (See the frontispiece photo.) Follow the arrow. This will put you on the Sam Merrill Trail. You'll hike through a ravine and then start a long ascent, complete with lots of switchbacks.

As you get close to the crest of Echo Mountain, you'll see signs that point to connector trails, including the path to Inspiration Point and Mount Lowe. You may want to leave those hikes for another day. Bear right to stay on the Sam Merrill Trail. When the path levels out, you'll be on Mount Lowe Railway Trail, the former bed of the long-gone railroad that brought visitors up the hillside from the valley below. Parts of the track, some giant gears, and pieces of an engine lie along the trail.

The story of Thaddeus Lowe, Echo Mountain House, and the Mount Lowe Railway is fascinating. If you're into history as much as hiking—and if you'd like to see some of what's waiting for you on the trail—check out an enlightening 4-minute video at youtube.com/watch?v=R1P6AaOy6mY.

Altadena Gravity Hill

To get to the Altadena Gravity Hill, head north on Lake Avenue off I-210. Turn right onto East Altadena Drive. Turn left onto Porter Avenue. Porter will end at East Loma Alta Drive. Turn left. The gravity hill begins in about 0.5 mile, shortly after you pass the second of two turnoffs for Sunny Oaks Circle.

Information for the Angeles National Forest is available by phone, Monday through Friday, at (626) 574-1613.

34

The Sturtevant Demons

Sturtevant Falls Trail, Angeles National Forest
Arcadia, Los Angeles County

STURTEVANT FALLS TRAIL is one of hundreds in the Angeles National Forest. It's easy to overlook this 3.0-mile out-and-back path in the 1,000 square miles of forest, but that would be a mistake. The hike has lots of spectacular photo ops, a creek, and a 50-foot waterfall. Who could ask for anything more?

Well, it would be nice if they got rid of the ghosts.

In the late summer, or whenever the Sturtevant Falls are dry, it may be best not to stand where the pool usually gathers at its base. According to an old wives' tale, thirsty demonic spirits will thrust their hands up through the arid soil and grab at you, clutching an ankle if possible, and try to pull you underground. Some people have described the creatures as looking like skeletons—dry as a bone!

Speaking of which, backpackers have claimed they've seen individual bones—and sometimes piles of them!—lying on the side of Sturtevant Falls Trail. Whether the remains are vestiges of the horrific subterranean creatures at the falls is unknown. Hikers also say they occasionally encounter extreme cold spots and dark, shadowy forms on the trail. Others have felt they were being watched by unseen eyes or have sensed a presence following them.

Elsewhere in the Angeles National Forest, motorists have reported coming upon hazy apparitions. The spectres will suddenly materialize on the road in front of the car and then vanish just before impact.

Haunted Trails

The moderate-difficulty hike to the Sturtevant Falls has been popular since the early twentieth century. The trail is almost always heavily trafficked. Besides hikers, leashed dogs and horses are allowed on the path. **Trailhead GPS: N34 11.730' / W118 01.350'**

To get to Sturtevant Falls trailhead, travel north on Santa Anita Avenue in Arcadia. (The street is exit 32 off I-210, which is also known as the Foothill Freeway.) As you reach the San Gabriel Mountains, the motorway narrows into Chantry Flats Road, also called Santa Anita Canyon Road. You'll follow this winding street uphill until it ends at the Chantry Flats parking lot. You'll need to have a National Forest Adventure Pass to park at the trailhead.

To access the trail, look for the paved service road that heads off to the right from the lower parking lot, just below the restrooms. You will descend 350 feet over the first 0.6 mile. This is a treat at the beginning of your walk, but the ascent is a killer on the way back.

After about 0.2 mile on this downward slope, you'll see a path on your right heading to the pools of Hermit Falls, but continue on the main trail. A mile into your hike, the pavement will end as the path swings to the right and crosses the Winter Creek Bridge. You'll see a man-made waterfall at this point, cascading over a concrete dam that was built in the 1960s by the Los Angeles Flood Control District.

Before long, the dirt trail will noticeably taper. The Big Santa Ana Creek will be to your right, and you'll be shaded by trees, mostly alder and oak. Ivy borders the trail. Your next landmark will be a signpost marked "#67 Castle on the Creek." The path turns slightly to the left and soon intersects Gabriella Trail at Fern Lodge Junction. Veer right to continue on Sturtevant Falls Trail.

As its name suggests, at Fiddler's Crossing you must cross the creek. **Fiddler's Crossing GPS: N34 12.564' / W118 01.092'**

You'll ford the stream two more times before you arrive at the falls. By the third crossing, you'll be able to hear the cascade. Keep going! It's just a few more yards until you get to Sturtevant Falls. The bucolic setting makes these waterfalls all the more special, and you'll no doubt spot several short stacks of stones (known as cairns) that were left behind by previous happy hikers.

Information for the Angeles National Forest is available by phone, Monday through Friday, at (626) 574-1613.

35

Spirited Sprites

Monrovia Canyon Waterfall Trail
Monrovia, Los Angeles County

F
EW TRAILS ARE as rewarding for so little effort as the short hike
to Monrovia Falls, even though the path may be haunted.

Monrovia is located east of Pasadena in the foothills of the
San Gabriel Mountains. The land was first inhabited by the
Tongva. The Spanish passed through in 1542, but it wasn't until
1771 that the Franciscans founded the Mission San Gabriel Arcangel.
After that, the Spanish referred to the Tongva as Gabrielino or Mission
Indians.

The city was incorporated in 1887 by prohibitionists who wanted a
"dry" community. From the 1920s to the 1960s, Monrovia was the home
of famed author Upton Sinclair. And in 1937 Patrick McDonald opened
a small restaurant called the Airdrome next to the Monrovia Airport. The
eatery eventually evolved into the fast-food behemoth McDonald's.

Monrovia has just over 37,000 inhabitants, but it boasts an 80-acre
public recreational area, Monrovia Canyon Park. It's located just 5 minutes
from downtown. This tranquil site is a relaxing oasis for the whole family, with easy walks for kids. There are picnic tables, barbecues, drinking
fountains, restrooms, handicapped parking spots, and rental campground
spaces. And, of course, there's Monrovia Falls, a 30-foot double cascade
that flows year-round.

Although there are many pleasant walkways in the park, the incidents of paranormal activity all seem to take place on the Waterfall Trail. Many hikers have reported feeling tiny bugs nipping at their flesh, even when there are no insects around. Bug spray won't keep the invisible entities off, nor will it make them stop biting. Neither does scratching or trying to brush them away. The attacks are worse for some people than others. Most victims only feel the inexplicable pinches, but a few have reported the sensation of mites burrowing into and crawling around under their skin. It's believed that the offenders are minute, unseeable sprites—or perhaps spirits—that are very possessive of the waterfalls and are trying to stop people from visiting them.

Haunted Trails

Of all the hikes possible in Monrovia Canyon Park, the most popular by far is the Monrovia Canyon Waterfall Trail. It's a moderately difficult, moderately trafficked 1.4-mile out-and-back path. The trail is partially paved, and dogs on leashes are allowed. The elevation gain to the falls is a mere 311 feet. **Trailhead GPS: N34 10.602' / W117 59.374'**

The most direct route to Monrovia Canyon Park from I-210 is to take exit 34 and travel north on Myrtle Avenue. Turn right on East Canyon Drive, and then bear right onto North Canyon Boulevard. This will take you to the parking lot for Monrovia Canyon visitors. The park is open to pedestrians from sunrise to 9 p.m. daily. The park is closed to vehicular traffic on Tuesday, but it's allowed other weekdays from 8 a.m. to 5 p.m. and Saturday and Sunday from 7 a.m. to 5 p.m. There is a parking fee.

Information for the Angeles National Forest is available by phone, Monday through Friday, at (626) 574-1613.

36

The Angeles National Forest

*East Fork Trail of the San Gabriel River, Crystal Lake Trail, South
Mount Hawkins Trail*
Azusa, Los Angeles County

NORMALLY A BRIDGE is thought of as little more than a way to get from here to there. But things get complicated when what lies on the other side *is* the Other Side, and the bridge allows spirits to return from the Great Beyond.

The infamous "Bridge to Nowhere" that spans the East Fork of the San Gabriel River was meant to be part of a road connecting the San Gabriel Valley with Wrightwood. When the span was constructed in 1936 there was a street leading up to it, but after a 1938 flood washed out the road, the whole project was abandoned. Now there's a dirt path leading up to the 103-foot-long bridge, and the span can be safely traversed by foot or mountain bike. Dogs are also allowed.

There are a couple of eerie old wives' tales about the Bridge to Nowhere. Some say it's a link to another dimension or a portal to the Next World. Occasionally people standing at one end of the bridge have seen a sparkling vortex at the other end, and they feel mysteriously and almost overwhelmingly drawn to it. If this happens to you, resist! Birds have been known to get sucked into the invisible whirlpool and disappear. The phenomenon is most active in the winter and after dark.

Legend has it that swimming or wading in the water beneath the bridge can cause temporary and even permanent amnesia. One survivor who got out of the water just in time said that as his memory faded, it felt as if some evil creature were feeding on his innermost thoughts, gaining more and more strength as his mind was being swept clean.

The Bridge to Nowhere isn't the only haunted site in this section of the San Gabriel Mountains. Crystal Lake Recreation Area is an easy getaway from Azusa. It's located in the San Gabriel Mountains on CA 39 just 26 miles north of the city at an elevation of about 5,550 feet. The park, administered by the USDA Forest Service, has a visitor center, a cafe and store, an amphitheater, and more than a hundred campsites. There are sixteen hiking trails and, of course, the lake. Part of the draw is that Crystal Lake is the only naturally formed lake in all of the San Gabriel Mountains.

Crystal Lake can be circled in such a short amount of time that it's hard to call it a hike. Likewise, the lake has shrunk so much since its heyday as a camping destination that it's sometimes generous even to call it a pond. Hopefully the water level will be high when you're there.

It certainly was in 1933 when the Civilian Conservation Corps built an open-air amphitheater and a dance hall as part of the New Deal. One of the work crew was Stephen Majors, who had ridden the rails into California looking for a job. Upon being hired to work at Crystal Lake, he sent for his wife, Heather, and their children, Susan, 12, and Markus, 10, to join him. Because he had a family, Majors was allowed to set up his tent some distance apart from the campsite for the single men.

On the night of September 19, 1934, Stephen and Heather returned from a walk to discover their tent had collapsed with their two youngsters trapped inside, screaming. Standing on top of the tarp was a grizzly bear, completely silent, trying to claw its way through the cloth. The parents shouted for help and then ran to fight the bear. By the time the crew chief and others arrived on the scene, all four family members were dead—disemboweled and torn limb from limb.

Although it certainly looked like a bear attack and had happened only minutes before the workers got there, the grizzly was nowhere to be seen. Construction was halted for two weeks while the men tried to track down the bear and kill it, but it was never found. The remains of the Majors family were buried on a nearby hillside.

Ever since, the phantoms of the four victims have been seen near the dance hall. They've continued to appear even after the lake's popularity waned and the building fell into ruin. It's hard to make out the spectres' features because they're more shadow than substance, but people can definitely make out four separate figures. They only materialize on or around September 19. It's believed that the family died so violently they may not know they're dead.

The stone dance floor is still intact, and almost every year on the anniversary of the bear attack, a few curiosity seekers camp out on it, hoping to catch a glimpse of the ghosts. In 1978 hundreds of people turned up to see the apparitions, and the spectres didn't disappoint. The otherworldly forms manifested under an oak tree about 30 feet from the dance studio and walked up the hillside before vanishing. The entire encounter lasted about 30 seconds.

It's always been assumed a grizzly bear killed the Majors family, even though no one witnessed the deaths and the last authenticated grizzly sighting in California had been in the early 1920s. In the way of myths, some paranormalists suggest it wasn't a flesh-and-blood bear that killed the Majors but an infernal spirit of some kind. Or was it something—or someone—else?

Only the Majors know for sure what happened to them. People say that ghosts of homicide victims often return to find or reveal their killers. Perhaps that's the real reason the Majors family still haunts the shore of Crystal Lake.

Finally, there's South Mount Hawkins. Both South Mount Hawkins and Mount Hawkins itself were named for Nellie Hawkins, who was a popular waitress at the long-gone Squirrel Inn, located on the North Fork of the San Gabriel River.

After the Curve Fire in 2002 destroyed the lookout tower on the summit of South Mount Hawkins, the USDA Forest Service stopped regular maintenance of the 7-mile dirt road from Crystal Lake up to where the observation post had stood. Nevertheless, hikers and mountain bikers find the road passable, if difficult, even with several sections of the path washed out or filled with boulders and rubble.

There are claims that evil spirits have lurked on the mountain ever since the forest fire. It's alleged that Satanists accidentally started the blaze while conducting demonic rites. As part of their rituals, they practiced animal sacrifices, mostly of birds, rabbits, and cats, and many misshapen revenants of those unfortunate creatures now roam the trails. Some people claim to have seen the ghostly figures of the occultists on the mountain as well. There's only one way to find out if such phantoms really exist on South Mount Hawkins. Take a hike!

Haunted Trails

The Bridge to Nowhere

The East Fork Trail to the Bridge to Nowhere is a 9.4-mile, moderate-difficulty out-and-back trek. You'll have plenty of company, because the path is heavily trafficked. It's a fun outing: There are several swimming holes along the way, including some under the bridge, and you'll have to cross the stream several times. There are some caveats: Parts of the trail are rocky, so make sure your boots are sturdy as well as waterproof. Oh, and bring bug spray. Also look out for poison oak on the shaded portions of the path. **Trailhead GPS: N34 14.205' / W117 45.54'**

To get there, follow the East Trail Road from Azusa until it ends at Coyote Flat. Parking is extremely limited at the entrance to the trail. Make sure your Adventure Pass is visible in your vehicle before you take off. Also, you'll need a Wilderness Permit to enter at the East Fork trailhead. Go through the gate on the northeast side of the lot, and start up the dirt road. When you get to a small picnic area and campground, ignore the turnoff to Heaton Fall. You want to stay on the main trail heading north. At about the 1.4-mile point, the path will briefly split into several branches, but they all head in the same direction and wind up at the same place.

Once the floodplain opens up, stay on the east bank of the stream, close to the canyon wall, and if there's a choice of an upper or lower level on the bluff, use the lower path. Always stay fairly close to the river and, when there's an option, follow the trail that shows the most use. Many of the trails that lead up the sides of the canyon simply dead-end, and if you accidentally take one you'll have to retrace your steps back down to the water.

There will be a path heading off to the northwest at about 1.65 miles. This is the never-completed Shoemaker Canyon Road, so don't take it. At this junction, you'll notice some patches of asphalt on the East Fork Trail from when it was a paved road. When you get to Allison Gulch, you'll have to cross the river **(N34 15.768' / W117 45.911').**

There will be at least three more crossings in the next 1.5 miles. You'll know you're getting close to the bridge when you see a prominent "Private Property" sign. It refers to the claim on a nearby mine, not the trail, so carry on. **Bridge to Nowhere GPS: N34 16.997' / W117 44.810'**

There are a few small trails near the bridge leading down to the water if you want to take a dip. The East Fork Trail does continue for a ways, and you might want to do a little more sightseeing before you head back to the trailhead. Hike as long as you like, but there's no overnight camping in the vicinity of the bridge.

Crystal Lake Trail

If you spend several days at the Crystal Lake Recreation Area, or at least stay overnight, your base will most probably be the Crystal Lake

Campgrounds. There's also a parking lot for day-trippers. Remember to place or hang your Adventure Pass where it can be seen easily. **Lot GPS: N34 19.444' / W117 50.055'**

Crystal Lake Trail is a 0.7-mile loop that, for the most part, hugs the lake's shoreline. It's of moderate difficulty and is moderately trafficked. Dogs are allowed on a leash. **Trailhead GPS: N34 19.155' / W117 50.692'**

South Mount Hawkins Trail

If you're already at Crystal Lake, you're in luck. There's an established loop trail that will take you to South Mount Hawkins and back. The first part of the hike, if taken counterclockwise via the Mount Hawkins Fire Road, is of moderate difficulty. The trail sets out from Deer Flats, just north of the Crystal Lake Campgrounds. **Trailhead GPS: N34 19.612' / W117 50.101'**

The turnaround point, if you decide not to complete the loop, is the summit of South Mount Hawkins. You would retrace your steps to the trailhead, making a 12.1-mile out-and-back hike. To finish the loop, continue from the summit onto Hawkins Ridge Trail, the Pacific Crest Trail, and Windy Gap Trail, giving you a round-trip of about 11 miles. This lightly trafficked second half of the loop is rated hard and should only be attempted by experienced hikers. **South Mount Hawkins Summit GPS: N34 18.705' / W117 48.627'**

Information for the Angeles National Forest is available by phone, Monday through Friday, at (626) 574-1613.

37

The Shadows of Thompson Creek

Thompson Creek Trail
Claremont, Los Angeles County

WITH STUNNING VIEWS of Mount Baldy, Thompson Creek Trail (also known as Thompson Creek Road Trail), is particularly popular with local residents. A model suburban hike, the paved trail follows a stream of the same name (actually a flood basin wash) that runs through a residential neighborhood. Even though it's a paved "city walk," Thompson Creek Trail is bordered by wildflowers, trees, and shrubs. As for fauna, you may see some deer, as well as quail and other birds. The trail is kid friendly, and dogs on leash are welcome, as are mountain bikes.

You wouldn't think such a pathway would be haunted. It's not in some mysterious, dark backwoods. It's so open and accessible. But there are multiple accounts of hikers encountering all sorts of paranormal activity, often in broad daylight. Folks have heard unexplainable scratching and scraping noises on the walkway, cracking in the bushes along its sides, and footsteps, both on the path and in the foliage—even when there's no sign of animals or people. Many hikers have encountered an impenetrable wall of fog. Try as they might, they couldn't get around or through it. They had to wait for the mist to dissipate or turn around. Some people have observed skull-like shapes in the clouds overhead, had visions of floating rocks, or passed trees that seemed to bleed.

Thompson Creek Trail from the Mountain Avenue entry point.
PHOTO COURTESY OF TOM OGDEN

The trail begins to get really spooky at dusk. Folks out for an early-evening stroll or a cool night jog—with nary a thought of ghosts on their minds—sometimes see "shadow people" looking down from the trees or following them on the path, just close enough to feel uncomfortable. Occasionally there are also hushed, almost imperceptible voices in the wind, urgently pleading for help.

With any luck you'll be there when the path is peaceful. When the ghosts are around, a jaunt down Thompson Creek Trail can be unsettling—a true walk on the wild side.

Haunted Trails

The full length of Thompson Creek Trail is 2.2 miles, end to end, but there are numerous entrance points along the easy, moderately-trafficked walkway. The nominal trailhead is on North Mills Road, just north of its intersection with Mount Baldy Road. There's a parking lot, but a fee must be paid on-site. The path has no restroom facilities. **Trailhead GPS: N34 08.530' / W117 42.428'**

There's another lot at the Indian Avenue trail entrance, which also has a fee that has to be paid on-site. There's limited free parking for this entrance in the La Puerta Sports Park lot across the street. Parking in the trail lot on Mountain Avenue requires a city permit, which must be purchased in advance. Most of the street parking anywhere near the trail requires a residential permit. Just make sure to check signage wherever you leave your car. Fines in the area are very high. Park rangers patrol the lots regularly, and presumably city traffic officers check street parking as well.

Inland Empire

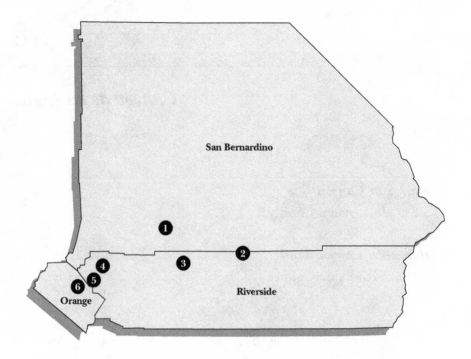

1 Big Falls
Forest Falls

2 Cap Rock and Gram Parsons Nature Trail
Joshua Tree National Park

3 Suicide Rock Trail
Idyllwild

4 Mount Rubidoux
Riverside

5 Horsethief Canyon Trail
Corona

6 Black Star Canyon
Silverado

38

Canyon de los Indios

Black Star Canyon
Silverado, Orange County

Horsethief Canyon Trail
Corona, Riverside County

DARK, HOODED FIGURES and furtive movements in the brush along the path are common sightings along Black Star Canyon Trail, which many consider to be the most actively "haunted hike" in California. There are no definite connections between the entities in the canyon and anyone who ever lived—or died—there, but the possible links between the remote chasm and the Next World are well worth contemplating.

Black Star Canyon cuts into the Santa Ana Mountains east of Irvine in Orange County. The Tongva people were the first residents of the gorge. Archaeological evidence suggests they didn't live there year-round, however. Rather, they would come into the mountain passes during the summer to escape the heat or to gather acorns, which was one of their primary foods.

When Spaniards (later the Mexicans) arrived, they called the place Cañada de los Indios, meaning "Canyon of the Indians." It received its current name after coal was discovered in the canyon in the 1870s, and the Black Star Coal Mining Company was established to extract it. The name was kept even after the Black Star operation closed. Although the mines themselves are long gone, some abandoned shafts, a few small piles of coal, and bits of metal scrap from the machinery can still be seen on the canyon floor.

Two infamous incidents in the past may contribute to the many hauntings in the canyon. In the early 1820s Shoshone in the upper gorge began to raid the Spanish ranchos outside the canyon to steal their horses. A way to stop the horse thieves came in 1831 when a group of trappers led by William Wolfskill arrived from New Mexico. The rancheros hired them to guide them to the Shoshone so they could take back their live-stock and exact revenge. Wolfskill led the rancheros into the canyon, and legend says the Shoshone were in the act of eating one of the horses when the rancheros found them. Wolfskill and the men annihilated the Native Americans, with only a few Shoshone escaping. The rancheros took back their horses and left the canyon.

The second episode was a murder trial in 1899. An argument between Henry Hungerford, a local landowner, and James Gregg, who had been hired to drive his livestock, led to a gunfight in which Gregg was mortally wounded. At trial Hungerford was found guilty of murder, but Judge J. W. Ballard ruled the prosecution didn't provide enough evidence to justify the verdict and granted an appeal. With no further proof at hand, the case was dropped, and Hungerford went free. The public was so upset with the judge's decision that they voted him out of office in the next election.

So what sort of spooky goings-on might Black Star Canyon hikers encounter? Visitors frequently detect the sound of screaming, howls, and Native American chanting, all thought to be ghosts of the Indian massacre of 1831. Even the remains of the mine shafts are allegedly haunted by the slaughtered Shoshone. There are also sudden gusts of wind and strange, inexplicable lights that flash in the canyon and the sensation of being touched. And then there are the dark human forms, or "shadow people."

The spirits of Gregg, Hungerford, and Ballard are all said to be spend-ing eternity in the canyon. If that weren't enough, urban legend has it that

Black Star Canyon was also the site of satanic rituals, witchcraft covens, and KKK meetings.

As with most hikes, you probably shouldn't venture into Black Star Canyon on your own. But then, you won't really be alone, will you?

The city of Corona is only 8 miles from Black Star Canyon, but they're not exactly neighbors. Corona is in Riverside County on the other side of the Santa Ana Mountains, and its Horsethief Canyon Trail is actually a paved service street up to a large, city water tower on top of a hill.

Those taking the path sometimes experience headaches, dizziness, nausea, or cold spots, all attributed to spectral presences, and they may hear phantom footsteps on the pavement behind them. There are a few apparitions on the trail as well. A Woman in White, described as a blonde in some sources, has drifted by hikers, and black, hazy forms are seen at the water tower itself. There are several intersecting dirt paths on the far side of the tower, including some that are wooded. Spectres have been seen darting around the groves at night, especially within one particular circle of trees. The phantoms love the dark, and people carrying flashlights have been shoved or kicked until they turned them off.

Haunted Trails

Black Star Canyon Trail
Black Star Canyon Trail is a 6.8-mile out-and-back path of mostly moderate difficulty. Although going off track isn't banned, it's probably safest to keep to the main route. With moderate to heavy traffic, the trail ends at a waterfall. Most people complete the round trip in about 5 hours. Dogs and horses are allowed on the path, but the final push to the falls becomes very difficult, even dangerous for them. **Trailhead GPS: N33 45.837' / W117 40.669'**

Black Star Canyon Road was originally a fire trail built by the USDA Forest Service in the 1920s. It branches off Silverado Canyon Road and ends at a gate, which is the pedestrian entrance and trailhead to the canyon. Although you will see "Private Property" and "No Trespassing" signs, these are unofficial and have been posted by squatters and locals who want to keep people out. Orange County and the forest service have allowed free right-of-passage on the road for decades, and Black Star Canyon itself has been a public park since 2011.

There's no parking lot at the trailhead, but there's usually ample parking along the sides of Black Star Canyon Road. Cars must park at least 50 feet away from gate on the east side of the road and 400 feet away on the west side of the street. Overnight parking is prohibited from 10 p.m. to 4 a.m.

The trail starts out wide, flat, and easy to negotiate. Once paved, the path is now a mostly hard-packed gravel-and-dirt road. Shortly into your hike, the track will begin to slope down until it reaches a small creek. Follow the brook upstream all the way to the falls.

You will have to cross the creek a couple of times, but it's usually narrow enough that you can easily jump over it. About 0.75 mile from the falls, the trail ascends sharply. There will soon be a lot of stones underfoot. Most are flat and can be negotiated without any problem, but they can be very slippery. There are also some boulders that are so large you will have to climb over them. A few have had ropes attached to help hikers pull themselves up. Continue following the creek to the falls. Other than the stream, the trail is not otherwise marked.

A couple of cautions and tips: Poison oak is everywhere! Find a photo to see what it looks like so you can avoid the shrub as much as possible. Long sleeves and long pants are recommended. If you have the option, wear hiking shoes or boots instead of running shoes, sneakers, or other footwear. There will be mud, and your feet will get wet, especially if you hike in the rainy season. (On the plus side, the creek and falls are at their fullest after a heavy rain.) Finally, bring your own drinking water despite there being a stream, especially during the summer months.

Horsethief Canyon Trail

Horsethief Canyon Trail is off Mountain Road in a neighborhood south of downtown Corona. It has a gate to prevent unauthorized motorized traffic from driving up to the tower, but it's okay to walk there. There will be no shade. The trailhead is unmarked. **Trailhead GPS: N33 43.196' / W117 26.018'**

The most direct route from Silverado to Corona is a 20-plus-mile drive up and around the mountain ridge, traveling north on CA 24 (which is a toll road) and then east on CA 91 (the Riverside Freeway). Corona lies at the intersection of CA 91 and a section of I-15 known as the Corona Freeway.

39

The Riverside Revenant

Mount Rubidoux Trail
Riverside, Riverside County

MOUNT RUBIDOUX, LOCATED on the Santa Ana River, is a Riverside landmark, primarily because of the monumental cross that's been on its summit since 1907. Frank A. Miller, who had recently opened the well-known Mission Inn hotel—itself a haunted site—purchased the hill. The small mountain was named for Louis Rubidoux, who had received the property from Mexico as a land grant.

Miller had a road constructed to the top of Mount Rubidoux, realizing that a trip to the summit could be a tourist destination. He erected the giant cross in honor of Father Junipero Serra, the founder the California missions. Easter sunrise services have been held at the foot of the cross since 1909. The hill's Peace Tower and Friendship Bridge were constructed in 1925, and the two stone structures were dedicated to Miller after his death in 1935 to honor his vision of global peace and cooperation.

For almost a century there have been urban legends of apparitions and secret tunnels on Mount Rubidoux. The spectres are seen standing near the cross, mostly at night of course. One of the spirits may be Miller himself, but several people have claimed that the ghost is holy and none other than Jesus Christ. Phantom cars, old-fashioned wagons, and bicycles are known to pass hikers on their way to the top. (Don't hitchhike!)

Some folks say the small rock cairns that dot the hillside somehow stack themselves. Still others believe that ghostly hands are piling up the stones. According to an old wives' tale, however, the mounds are built by elves or tiny people. The mystic creatures most often appear between the hours of 1 a.m. and 3 a.m., and they travel in groups of three, running and hiding as if playing some sort of game. They will throw small rocks at you if they see you, and then later they'll use them to make little cairns on any trails or places you've walked.

Perhaps the wildest legend about Mount Rubidoux is that Miller dug catacombs in the sides of the mountain and somehow bored a secret tunnel all the way from the top of the hill to the bowels of the Mission Inn. No trace of an underground crypt or passageway has ever been found.

According to a popular ghost story, the nearby Evergreen Memorial Historic Cemetery is also haunted. It's located at 14th and Pine Streets at the foot of Mount Rubidoux, and Frank Miller is one of the graveyard's "residents." Could he also be one of the ghosts on his beloved hilltop?

Haunted Trails

There are many trails to the summit of Mount Rubidoux, and a portion of the Santa Ana River Walk runs along its base. Mount Rubidoux Trail is probably the easiest to the top. It's a heavily trafficked 2.7-mile loop that offers panoramic views of the Riverside area, as well as a close-up visit to the mound's landmark cross. The walkway is mostly paved. The hike is considered to be kid friendly, and dogs on a leash can join in on the fun. There is no shade on the trail, so wear sunscreen and bring a hat. Finding parking at the trailhead can be difficult, but there is plenty at nearby Ryan Bonaminio Park. The trailhead is located off Glenwood Drive. **Trailhead GPS: N33 58.773' / W177 23.521'**

40

Big Bite

Big Falls
Forest Falls, San Bernardino County

T HERE'S AN OLD wives' tale that a ruthless female wraith attacks visitors to Big Falls, biting into them with her rotted teeth. You're in no danger, though, if you stay out of the water. She apparently lurks beneath the surface of the pool at the bottom of the cascades and grabs at potential victims, either as they make their way along the submerged rocks or when they stop to gaze up at the falls.

But the hike to Big Falls is worth the risk. The best time to visit is during the spring and summer months. Even though the falls are in Southern California, you'll be at an elevation of 6,000 feet. There will most probably be snow and ice in the winter and into the early spring. The road to the falls is closed if it's impassible.

The trail to the falls is short, but it becomes steep as it approaches the terraced cascades—at points up to an 85 percent grade! The main path leads to the base of the lower falls, and once you're there you'll see trails that lead to higher viewpoints of the upper falls. But be careful: The rocks around Big Falls are always slick, and many of them are loose. Climbing them at any time can be downright dangerous—even though you'll be safe from the clutches of the water witch.

Haunted Trails

Big Falls Trail is just one of more than 150 established hiking paths in the San Bernardino Forest. The easy 0.7-mile out-and-back trail is located just outside the community of Forest Falls. The path is said to be moderately trafficked, but it can easily become very crowded. Leashed dogs are allowed. **Trailhead GPS: N34 04.940' / W116 53.620'**

An Adventure Pass is required to park in the paved lot. There's also a gravel area behind the main lot where parking is free, but it tends to fill quickly. Check with a ranger or at the visitor center before leaving your car on the side of the road. Speaking of which, during flash floods or the rare heavy rains, the streets near the parking lots can be washed out.

41

The End

Suicide Rock Trail
Idyllwild, Riverside County

ACKPACKERS OFTEN CHOOSE remote, secluded trails, but that doesn't mean they want to disappear forever—especially at their own hands.

Suicide Rock in Mount San Jacinto State Park got its name from an ancient Native American myth in which two young Cahuilla lovers threw themselves to their death from the 7,510-foot summit rather than be separated by their families. (Shades of Romeo and Juliet!) The landmark's name was originally Suicide Peak, but it was changed in the 1940s when geologists determined the stone sentinel isn't a separate mountain but merely a rocky outcrop.

A more recent legend about the path up to the lookout has nothing to do with the Cahuilla couple. Instead, paranormalists say that a sinister entity haunts the aptly named Suicide Rock Trail. It causes hikers to experience sudden, overwhelming feelings of hopelessness and gloom, sometimes to the point that they want to take their own lives.

Several hikers have seen the cryptic being that causes these perilous moods. They say their encounter with the sinister spirit started with the strange sensation of being followed. When they turned to look back, they found themselves staring into a pair of large, black eyes—seemingly boring straight into their souls! Whatever the creature was—ghost or

Suicide Rock, Mount San Jacinto State Park.
PHOTO COURTESY OF CHRISTINE COX

demon—they heard it softly growl, "Time to die!" followed by an evil, maniacal laugh. Then the panic set in, the crushing melancholy, the urge to end it all. It took superhuman willpower for the backpackers to conquer the suicidal impulse and escape.

A lot of hikers stop short of climbing to the summit of Suicide Rock, opting instead to enjoy the landscape from its base and the trail's many clearings. The path does continue to the top, however, and many adventurers will want to make the final push. Whatever you choose to do—and

Suicide Rock Trail, Mount San Jacinto State Park.
PHOTO COURTESY OF CHRISTINE COX

this shouldn't have to be said—don't get too close to the edge of a cliff! Suicide Rock is only a name, not a recommendation.

Haunted Trails

To hike to Suicide Rock, start from the Deer Springs trailhead, which is located midway between Idyllwild and Pine Cove on CA 243 (also known as the Banning-Idyllwild Panoramic Highway). **Deer Springs Trailhead GPS: N33 45187' / W166 43.358'**

From the trailhead, you'll hike a series of switchbacks until you reach a junction at about the 2.3-mile point. Turn right, following the sign to Suicide Rock. It will be another mile or so to your destination. All along the trail there are viewpoints that allow to you see across Strawberry Valley over to Lily Rock, Tahquitz Peak, and two higher crests, Jean Peak and Marion Mountain.

Suicide Rock Trail is very popular and is heavily trafficked during all seasons. Each time of the year has its advantages and drawbacks. Late spring through early fall can be warm and sunny but dry and dusty. Mid-autumn through early spring will be chilly if not downright cold. There also may be rain, and in the winter you will almost certainly be hiking through at least a little snow. The path is of moderate difficulty. The slope is almost continuous, though seldom over a grade of 20 percent. The trail is approximately 6.5 miles out and back. Dogs are not allowed.

There's a large dirt parking area on the north side of the road at the trailhead. The lot tends to fill in the summer, so start out early if you want to make sure you'll find a spot.

Most of Mount San Jacinto State Park has been designated as wilderness, so if you don't have a wilderness permit, stop at the park ranger station outside of Idyllwild to get one. They're free.

42

Gram's Ghost

J OSHUA TREE NATIONAL Park is located near Twentynine Palms, about 50 miles outside Palm Springs, and it straddles San Bernardino and Riverside Counties. Originally designated a national monument in 1936, Joshua Tree became a national park as part of the California Desert Protection Act passed by Congress in 1994. The park is immense, larger than the state of Rhode Island. It contains 790,636 acres, of which 429,690 acres are designated wilderness. The park receives close to 3 million visitors a year.

The park is named for its unique flora, the Joshua tree (*Yucca brevifolia*), which is native to the Mojave Desert. The trees grow both in small clusters and as single, isolated plants. Ranging in height from 15 to 40 feet, Joshua trees are not actually trees or cacti. Rather, they're members of the agave family. The tree's distinguishing feature is that its trunk splits into several upwardly raised arms, which then also split numerous times. Most of the branches end in a bunch of spiky green leaves that resembles a bottlebrush. (In addition to Joshua trees, the park supports a variety of pine, juniper, and oak trees, desert shrub, and other flowering flora.)

Joshua Tree National Park is also known for its many monzogranite rock formations, many of which have been given imaginative names, such as Skull Rock, Cyclops, and Pee Wee. The larger boulders are especially popular with rock climbers and scramblers. The best known of these megaliths is probably Cap Rock due to its association with singer/songwriter/musician Gram Parsons.

Parsons combined traditional song styles to become one of the pioneers of what is now known as folk rock, alternative country, or country rock. Parsons preferred to call his new sound "Cosmic American Music." He founded one group, the International Submarine Band, and cofounded another, the Flying Burrito Brothers. In 1968 he recorded with the Byrds, although technically he was never a full member. Parsons later became a close friend of Keith Richards, and for the last two years of his life, Parsons toured with Emmylou Harris.

As the frenzied 1960s came to a close, Parsons fell in love with the peace and solitude he discovered at Joshua Tree. His favorite location in the park was Cap Rock, where he would meditate while staring into the starry sky. He allegedly often indulged in "pharmaceuticals," which may or may not help explain the many UFO sightings he claimed to have had. (Parsons is far from the only person to have claimed that UFOs frequent Joshua Tree, however.)

On September 17, 1973, Parsons sought out the solace of Joshua Tree to recharge his batteries prior to setting out on an announced October tour. During the getaway, he reportedly consumed enormous amounts of barbiturates and alcohol. He was staying at the Joshua Tree Inn, and on his last night there he downed six double tequilas in front of friends. Then, a woman whose identity remains unknown, purportedly followed him to his room (Room 8) and injected him with morphine. Cut to the chase: Parsons was declared DOA at High Desert Memorial Hospital in Yucca Valley just after midnight on September 19. He was 26.

The rest of the Parsons story sounds stranger than fiction. The musician had always told his friend Phil Kaufman that after his death he wanted to be cremated in Joshua Tree and have his ashes scattered on Cap Rock. Gram's stepfather wanted his remains back in New Orleans, though. That didn't deter Kaufman. With security being much different in 1973, he and a friend were able to drive into Los Angeles International

Cap Rock, Joshua Tree National Park.
PHOTO COURTESY OF CRAIG TYLER

Airport in a borrowed hearse and abscond with Parsons's body, already in its casket ready for shipment.

Kaufman and his friend reached Cap Rock, lugged the coffin close to the mammoth outcrop, poured 5 gallons of gasoline onto the corpse, and threw in a match. The resultant fireball alerted the police. The men escaped but were arrested two days later. There seemed to be no felony law against stealing a body, so they were only fined $750 for theft of the casket. No charges were filed for abandoning the burnt remains. What was left of Parsons was sent to Louisiana, but certainly some of the airborne ashes made their way over to Cap Rock.

Apparently Parsons's spirit remained behind as well. Many visitors have spotted his ghost at Cap Rock, and his apparition also turns up at the motel where he died. Rangers at Joshua Tree National Park are allowed to decide for themselves whether to mention Parsons on their tours.

Shortly after his death, Parsons's fans marked the cremation site with a small concrete slab. (It has since been relocated to the Joshua Tree Inn.) Folks still leave behind flowers and burnt joints or make tiny rock cairns in the park to honor Parsons.

The spectre of Gram Parsons won't hurt you in Joshua Tree National Park, but don't think you're completely safe. Ancient Navajo legends tell of the *yee naagloshii*, or "he who walks on all fours." They are demonic shape-shifters who were once shamans or "medicine men" that used their abilities for evil. In the park, they take the form of common desert animals such as coyotes or wolves to prey on the living. Campers hear the creatures' eerie howls in the night just before they attack. There have been many mysterious deaths in Joshua Tree National Park, and even more people have gone missing, but, not surprisingly, the mythic skinwalkers are never listed as the official cause.

Haunted Trails

Cap Rock Trail is an easy, lightly trafficked 0.3-mile path that completely encircles the huge stone formation. The Gram Parsons Nature Trail, a flat 0.4-mile, oval-shaped loop, has recently been attached to Cap Rock Trail. As seen from above, the two trails form a sort of figure eight. **Trailhead GPS: N33 59.344' / W116 09.838'**

Care to spend the night in Joshua Tree Inn? It's located just 5 miles outside the entrance to the national park at 61259 Twentynine Palms Hwy., Joshua Tree, CA 02252. Phone (760) 366-1188. If you dare, ask to stay in Room 8. But don't be too disappointed: When last checked, the only piece of furniture in the room dating to the night of Parsons's death was a round mirror at the foot of the bed.

Greater San Diego

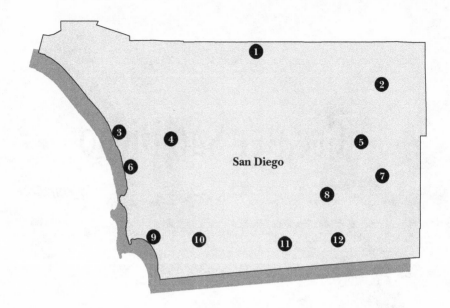

43

The Whisperer

Thunder Spring and Chimney Flats Loop Trail, Palomar Mountain State Park
Palomar Mountain, San Diego County

PALOMAR MOUNTAIN IS located in northern San Diego County in the Peninsular Ranges between Southern California and Baja. The Luiseno peoples that once inhabited the region called the mountain "Paauw," so it's possible that its current name is merely a corruption of the native word. In Spanish, however, the word "Palomar" translates as "pigeon roost," and at the time of colonization, Palomar Mountain was home to hundreds, probably thousands, of band-tailed pigeons.

The mountain ridge is, perhaps, most famous as the location of the Palomar Observatory and the Hale Telescope. At 200 inches in diameter, Hale Telescope was the largest in the world from 1949 to 1992. The observatory is still an important astronomical research facility.

Although they're located within Palomar Mountain State Park, the observatory and much of the property immediately surrounding it are not open to the general public. The west side of the park, which can be visited, welcomes about 70,000 people per year. It's heavily forested with pine, cedar, and oak as well as copious ferns.

One of the park's trails, the Thunder Spring and Chimney Flats Loop Trail, is known for its ghosts. A late nineteenth-century legend has it that a local man by the name of "Big Willy" Pearson was injured in the woods near Doane Pond while hunting in the snow. He saw a cabin ahead in the woods, so even though he didn't know the owner, he made his way there to seek help. Surprisingly, the place was empty. Nevertheless, it was getting dark, and he needed rest and shelter, so Big Willy made himself at home.

Or he would have—if it hadn't been a haunted house. All through the night, he was pestered by nonstop spooky, disembodied whispering. Big Willy fled at daybreak, and before long he moved far away. Many years later, in the 1880s, he returned to visit the site of his night of horror, hoping to confront his fear and rid himself of the memory. But the trip was cut short: As he neared the house, a huge branch from a black oak tree snapped off without warning, fell, and killed him instantly.

Today, folks walking the Thunder Spring and Chimney Flats Loop Trail sometimes hear the same sort of whispers that terrorized Big Willy. Most of the hikers chalk it up to the wind, but a few have claimed they heard their names being called in the breeze.

Young children and seniors who hike the trail have an even more disturbing paranormal phenomenon to worry about. If they hear the otherworldly voice murmuring their name, they might also experience dreadful visions of crushed and rotting corpses.

It's always important to remember that contact of any kind with the Spirit World is extremely rare. When you hike through Palomar Mountain State Park, however, you could be one of the exceptions.

Haunted Trails

Thunder Spring and Chimney Flats Loop Trail, a 3.85-mile path, is of moderate difficulty and is moderately trafficked. The trailhead is located at the southern end of the parking lot for Doane Pond. **Trailhead GPS: N33 20.492' / W116 54.081'**

The path splits just before you reach the pond. Bear left around the eastern side of the lake onto Thunder Spring Trail. (If you bear right, you'll go onto Chimney Flats Trail.)

After you pass the pond, Doane Creek will be on your left. About 0.6 mile into the walk, you'll see a small stream of water flowing out of the hillside on your right. This is Thunder Spring. Continue walking through the forest. At about the 1-mile mark of the hike, Upper Doane Valley Trail will branch off to the left, but don't take it! Stay on Thunder Spring Trail. After another 0.5 mile or so, the woods will open up to reveal a large meadow. This is Chimney Flats, and it's at this point the path becomes Chimney Flats Trail.

At 2.65 miles into the hike, the path will "T." Turning left and staying on Chimney Flats Trail will lead you back to the trailhead. Consider turning right to take a 0.1-mile detour to see what little is left of Scott's cabin, which is ground zero for the hauntings. You'll find a clearing where a square outline of logs and grooves in the ground mark the spot that the old nineteenth-century homesteader's house used to stand.

There are well-maintained campgrounds in Palomar Mountain State Park, but reservations are highly recommended (ReserveCalifornia.com). There's a day-use fee for vehicles, but not for hikers. Mountain bikes and dogs, even on a leash, are not allowed on the trails.

44

Denizens of the Desert

Borrego Springs, Borrego Sink, Borrego Palm Canyon Trail, Carrizo Wash
Borrego Springs, San Diego County

Ghost Mountain, Tierra Blanco Canyon, Moonlight Canyon Trail
Anza-Borrego Desert State Park, San Diego County

A T MORE THAN 600,000 acres, Anza-Borrego Desert State Park is the largest state park in California. In fact, it takes up a full 20 percent of San Diego County. The park is located within California's Colorado Desert, which itself is part of the Sonoran Desert. Yes, there are a few sand dunes, but there are also springs and oases, grasslands, brush, and a wide range of desert wildlife. The topography is just as varied, from its lowest point, the Salton Sea, to mountain peaks in the Peninsular Ranges nearly 10,000 feet in height.

The park gets the first part of its name from Juan Bautista de Anza, an eighteenth-century Spanish explorer who traveled through the region. As for *borrego*, the Spanish word translates as "sheep," and the park is home to the now-endangered peninsular bighorn sheep. Hiking opportunities in and around Anza-Borrego Desert State Park are as endless as the ghost sightings.

The community of Borrego Springs lies just outside the northeast boundary line of the park. Back around the time of the California gold rush, a raconteur named Thomas Long Smith moved to the West from Kentucky and reinvented himself as Peg Leg Smith. He told the story far and wide that he had discovered gold nuggets in the Borrego Springs area. The problem was, he couldn't remember the location. He never found it again—if the gold had ever existed in the first place. Neither did any of the dozens, perhaps hundreds, of prospectors that went into the hills searching for it. Today the rascal is remembered as "Liar" Peg Leg Smith and is memorialized as such on a monument just outside of town.

It's not Peg Leg's ghost that haunts Borrego Springs, however. The spectre is an 8-foot-tall skeleton with a glowing white orb where its heart should be. The spirit has shown up since the 1860s, and legend has it that he's there to guard the gold.

Borrego Sink is a dry ravine about 4.5 miles to the southeast of Borrego Springs in the Borrego Badlands. Since the late 1930s, campers in the gorge have complained of being disturbed—and more than a little frightened—by apelike beasts with red eyes and white hair, known in Native American folklore as Hairy Ghosts. Fortunately, backpackers have always been able to keep the beasts at bay.

The Carrizo Badlands are found in the southeastern corner of Anza-Borrego Desert State Park. Carrizo Creek flows from the hills in the Badlands, tapers off, and ends as it reaches Imperial Valley. The resulting dry creek bed, the Carrizo Wash, is located just 3 miles east of where the Carrizo Stage Station once stood. The dusty wash parallels the Old Butterfield Road, which was a major stagecoach route in the mid-nineteenth century.

Despite the fact that almost all stagecoach travel through the Carrizo Corridor had ended by the 1870s—the Transcontinental Railroad was completed in 1869—modern-day hikers in the Carrizo Wash occasionally see unmistakable yet inexplicable ruts formed by wagon wheels. From time to time, folks actually see the ghost of a coach barreling down the road. Also many backpackers who camp overnight between Carrizo Wash and Agua Caliente report hearing a runaway stagecoach filled with panicked passengers. Apparently the distinctive sounds go back to a bungled holdup in the 1860s in which the outlaws shot the stagecoach driver, but the horses didn't stop, dragging the wagon into the desert.

Ghost Mountain is located within Anza-Borrego Desert State Park. The peak was named by artist and author Marshal South, who built a house (which he called Yaquitepec) on a high ridge. He would often refer to the paths that led to his home as "thin, ghost trails." He lived there with his wife and three children from 1930 until 1947, when the marriage ended in divorce. South died the following year.

The adobe house has fallen apart, but it's still there. A man who camped overnight near the ruins claimed that he heard the slamming of a nonexistent door as well as strangers outside his tent chatting in a weird language. These phenomena were followed by the brief sound of a beating drum, and then a woman howling and hissing. Another backpacker reported seeing the apparition of a Native American, which isn't surprising, since Cahuilla folklore says the desert is filled with spirits.

For many years, a phantom Viking ship was seen sticking out of a mountainside in Tierra Blanco Canyon, high above Aqua Caliente Springs. Its appearance is, perhaps, linked to a Mayo and Seri tribal myth from the Mexican state of Sonora, which lies across the US border south of Anza-Borrego Desert State Park.

Their legends tell of a ship that arrived in the distant past from a faraway land across the sea. The boat supposedly had a bow shaped like a snake, which to modern ears sounds a lot like an ancient Norse vessel. We know that Vikings reached North America on the Atlantic shore. Is it possible they made it to Baja as well? Unfortunately, the ghost ship hasn't been seen since 1933, when a major earthquake hit the region.

We can't leave Anza-Borrego Desert State Park without mentioning the Borrego Sandman, its mysterious cryptid inhabitant. Most people recognize it by its more common name: Bigfoot.

The California Sasquatch is usually associated with remote, forested areas, but there have been reports of apelike creatures throughout the state. In the 1950s and 1960s, for example, a Bigfoot was seen so often by spectators at Mickey Thompson's Fontana International Dragway that they nicknamed it the "Speedway Monster." It didn't always stay at the racetrack, however. In 1965 the beast surprised a young Fontana man as he was walking home and tore at the guy's clothing; that same year, a Sasquatch reached through the open window of a parked car, terrifying its driver, a woman named Jerri Mendenhall. (It's unknown whether these encounters were all with the same Bigfoot.)

In the 1970s several Sasquatch showed up in the Lancaster-Palmdale area at Edwards Air Force Base. The creatures were spotted through night-vision binoculars and captured on security cameras as they prowled the perimeter of the base, walked onto its grounds, and entered underground tunnels. If footage exists of them, it is undoubtedly classified.

Bigfoot also roams the desert areas of California, and their presence has been known for centuries. The Native Americans warned the first Spanish missionaries to stay far away from the foul-smelling monstrosities, which they called "Hairy Devils." According to the local tribes, the hideous man-apes lived along the Santa Ana River at a spot they called *towis puki*, or the "Camp of the Devil."

In the late 1800s there was a rash of Bigfoot sightings around Deadman's Hole, which was a stagecoach stop just a few miles west of Anza-Borrego Desert State Park. The claims increased during a spate of mysterious deaths in the area in which the victims were torn apart, as if by wild animals.

The first published account of a Hairy Devil was in the *San Diego Union* in April 1876. A man named Turner Helm said that he and a fellow prospector were at Warner's Ranch near Deadman's Hole when they ran into a Sasquatch, which Helm described as having a long, dark beard and black, dense hair on its head. In fact, its entire body was covered in coarse fur like a bear. At first, the creature was seated on a stone but stood up to look at them when the strangers approached. As soon as the men aimed their rifles at it, the beast ran off.

In March 1888 the *San Diego Transcript* published a story about two hunters, Charles Cox and Edward Dean, who set out across the desert to track down the Hairy Devil, which they believed to be responsible for three murders at Deadman's Hole. The men claimed they were successful and shot the Bigfoot, allowing them to get a good look at it.

The creature was at least 6 feet tall, with 24-inch feet, had no tail, and was completely covered with deep brown hair. The men estimated its weight to be about 400 pounds. To the hunters, its face looked more Native American than European, but its teeth were jagged and fanged like those of a wild animal. The beast looked like a bear from the back. It had four legs, but it "walked" upright. The front "arms" were long enough to allow the creature to climb and run, much like a gorilla. Supposedly the men attempted to ship the strange animal's body to San Diego, but somehow the remains disappeared before anyone else could see them. (It's very likely their claims were a hoax.)

In 1939 several Sasquatch surrounded a prospector while he was camping near the Borrego Sink. He said the creatures were covered in white fur and had red eyes, similar to descriptions of the Himalayan yeti. The miner believed they only kept their distance because they were afraid of his campfire.

Then in 1964 a Sasquatch showered a father and son with small stones while they were hiking in Escondido, about 50 miles east of Borrego

Springs. That same year, three cows were found mutilated on the MGM Ranch near Jamul, west of Anza-Borrego Desert State Park. Conspiracy theorists blamed the cattle's slaughter on everyone from Satanists to aliens and the Borrego Sandman.

Also in 1964, Victor Stoyanow, a major in the US Marines, stumbled across a set of three-toed footprints, 14 inches long and 9 inches wide, close to Borrego Springs. Four years later, Harold Lancaster, a miner, saw a Bigfoot coming toward him in the Borrego Sink and had to shoot a pistol in the air to frighten it off. Both of the men's stories were published in a 1969 *SAGA* magazine article entitled "America's Terrifying Woodland Monster-men."

In 1993 a hiker ran into a Sasquatch in, of all places, a restroom on the La Jolla Indian Reservation. Two other backpackers discovered enormous, Bigfoot-like footprints in 1998 while hiking Boundary Peak near the Mexican border.

Reports of Bigfoot in the Borrego Sink and the Anza-Borrego Desert have died down in the last twenty years, but they've never completely stopped. Maybe you'll be the first to see the Borrego Sandman this millennium.

Of course, besides the ghosts and Bigfoot, Anza-Borrego Desert State Park is known for the hot springs in Aqua Caliente. None of the hikes in this chapter are too strenuous, but before leaving the park, you might consider treating yourself to a relaxing, therapeutic soak. You want to be refreshed before setting out on your next haunted hike, right?

Haunted Trails

Borrego Palm Canyon
The most popular hike in Anza-Borrego Desert State Park is the 2.9-mile moderately difficult trail into Borrego Palm Canyon. The heavily trafficked trail into the gorge follows Palm Canyon Creek out to an oasis filled

with palm trees. Dogs are prohibited on the path. **Trailhead GPS: N33 16.219' / W116 25.084'**

In winter and spring, be on the lookout for a waterfall (**N33 16.712' / W116 25.804'**) flowing from between the boulders on your right. There's also a waterfall in the grotto at the oasis. On your return trip, you may want to take the path that runs along the opposite side of the creek, creating a loop trail.

It's possible to continue into the canyon past the oasis by following the creek upstream. You'll discover the trees become more plentiful the farther you go into the ravine, but the trail also becomes increasingly difficult. The canyon splits in about 2 miles, and the trails are unmarked, so plan ahead if you think you want to extend your hike.

Carrizo Wash

There is no established trail through the Carrizo Wash. The Carrizo Stage Station stood at **N32 52.509' / W116 06.501'**. The wash extends slightly west and east of the historic site.

Ghost Mountain

You can visit the remains of Yaquitepec by way of a short but steep hike up Ghost Mountain. It's a moderately trafficked, 1.1-mile out-and-back trail of moderate difficulty. There's a parking lot at the trailhead. **Trailhead GPS: N33 00.190' / W116 23.383'**

Moonlight Canyon Trail

You can get good views of the Tierra Blanco Mountains from the Moonlight Canyon Trail. It's an easy, 1.6-mile, moderately trafficked loop starting at the Aqua Caliente Campground. **Trailhead GPS: N32 56.915' / W116 18.187'**

45

The Vallecito Visions

Yaqui Well, Volcan Mountain, Vallecito County Park
Julian, San Diego County

THE ARID, SPARSELY populated spaces around Julian can sometimes be inhospitable to the living, but the conditions don't seem to affect those who have returned from the Other Side.

Yaqui Well is a small seep located in the San Felipe Wash at the edge of the Anza-Borrego Desert State Park. It was first discovered by Native Americans, and it's thought to be named for a Yaqui woman from Sonora, Mexico, who once lived close to the well. In the nineteenth and early twentieth centuries, the spring was a welcome sight to settlers and others moving west, and sometime after 1909 a man named Paul Sentenac developed the surrounding area into a cattle ranch.

Besides the birds and flowers, one of Yaqui Well's major distinctions is its ghost, or rather ghosts. The apparitions of three men who died shortly after discovering gold in the region manifest at Yaqui Well at night, circling the watering hole hand in hand, dancing in glee.

On nearby Volcan Mountain, a phantom black horse, its innards hanging from its slit belly, gallops during the third week of every month. The stallion is followed by a parade of ethereal men and women with distorted faces who silently scream in agony. No one knows who these distressing spectres are or were, the circumstances of their deaths, or the reason they've returned to haunt the mountainside.

Also near Julian is the 77-acre Vallecito County Park. Its Spanish name, *vallecito*, means "little valley." Because of the plentiful water, the basin has been a stopover for hundreds of years, starting with the native Kumeyaay and followed by western pioneers.

There are forty-four camping sites in the park for tents, trailers, and motor homes. The park has picnic tables, fire rings, barbecue stoves, restrooms, and showers nestled among the low trees and chaparral. Otherwise, there are very few structures standing in Vallecito County Park. One exception is the reconstructed adobe that once served as a stagecoach way station.

At the time of the gold rush, there was only one wagon road from back East traveling through Southern California. It was referred to as the Great Southern Stage Route of 1849 (now County Route S2). When James R. Lassiter came through in 1851, he decided to stay in Vallecito to open a much-needed general store and campground. The venture was immediately successful. Soon other pioneers began to settle in the area, and the depot was made an official stop on the first regular mail route between San Diego and Yuma, Arizona.

Sometime in the mid- to late 1850s a woman named Eileen O'Conner arrived at the Vallecito station on the Butterfield Stage from back East. She was on her way to Sacramento to marry her fiancé, who had struck it rich as a prospector. She was very sick, however—so sick that she had to be carried from the stagecoach into the adobe's waiting room. The locals did everything they could for her, but she died two days later. She was dressed in the wedding gown they found in her trunk and buried in the small Campo Santo cemetery next to the depot.

Almost immediately, O'Conner's anxious ghost began to show up in the adobe, seemingly waiting for the next northern-bound stagecoach to appear. The haunting is said to continue. The adobe house you see today isn't Lassiter's original station, however. It dates to 1934 and is part replica, part restoration. The Lady in White, as Eileen's spirit is called, doesn't seem to care. She usually materializes after dark, so it's overnight campers and backpackers who see her most often.

She's not the only apparition who manifests in Vallecito County Park. Two other spectres seen in the immediate area belong to Buck and Roland, two outlaws from Texas who killed each other in a duel. On some nights you might catch a glimpse of a spectral stagecoach, complete with a driver, silently hurtling down the old Great Southern Stage Route.

There's one other wraith from the Old West wandering the hillsides above the adobe: the White Horse of Vallecito. The luminous steed once belonged to the leader of a gang of stagecoach robbers. A failed holdup attempt led to all four bandits being killed and the horse escaping. The stallion's spectre has returned to the scene of the action, where it usually appears around midnight on moonlit evenings.

There's an old saying that good things come in threes. Well, they certainly do in Julian. With Yaqui Well, Volcan Mountain, and Vallecito County Park all within a few miles of each other, you have three perfect places to encounter spooks.

Haunted Trails

Yaqui Well Nature Trail

The Yaqui Well Nature Trail is an easy, 1.64-mile out-and-back path that's only lightly trafficked. No permit or fee is required. It's a hiking trail only: No dogs or mountain bikes are allowed. The path is noted for the variety of plants as well as more than eighty species of birds. The hike is most comfortable from October through April. **Trailhead GPS: N33 08.321' / W116 22.550'**

The trail sets off from Yaqui Pass Road (S 3), which branches off from CA 78. The path is plainly marked and begins directly across the road from the Tamarisk Grove Campground. There's a free nature guide available at the signpost or at the campgrounds, with numbers in the pamphlet corresponding to fourteen scenic markers along the trail. (Before leaving, consider returning the nature guide for a future hiker's use.)

The hike begins as a singletrack over dirt and rock. You'll pass over a slight ridge dotted with teddy bear cacti, and then descend to the level San Felipe Wash. As you approach the well (number fourteen on your guide), the amount of flora increases substantially. Unfortunately, these days there is seldom if ever visible water at the seep.

Visitors are asked to leave the terrain unspoiled and not go beyond the well. On your outbound hike, you may have noticed a path that veered to the left just before you reached the well. If, on your return, you walk this trail for about 0.1 mile, you'll reach the Yaqui Well Primitive Campground. From there you can follow the dirt Grapevine Canyon Road for 0.2 mile back to the trailhead, making a loop.

Volcan Mountain Trail

Volcan Mountain Trail is located in the Volcan Mountain Wilderness Preserve. The 4.9-mile out-and-back path to the top of Volcan Mountain is of moderate difficulty and is moderately trafficked. The track is smooth and maintained, but there's a 1,227-foot gain in elevation. The grade can go as high as 20 percent on some portions of the trail. **Trailhead GPS: N33 06.306' / W116 36.139'**

To access the Volcan Mountain Trail, park on Farmer Road and pass through the Hubbell Gate. There's a viewing platform near the summit of Volcan Mountain, and on clear days it's possible to see as far as the Salton Sea. Volcan Mountain Wilderness Preserve is open daily from 8 a.m. to sunset. The preserve spans about 2,900 acres of mixed conifer forest.

If you'd rather take an "armchair hike" or simply want to see what the route looks like before you go, the County of San Diego has posted a video of the trail at countynewscenter.com/virtual-hike-volcan-mountain-summit.

Vallecito County Park and Stage Station

The restored stagecoach station is located in Vallecito County Park, about 4 miles northwest of Agua Caliente Springs. **Stage Station GPS: N32 58.554' / W116 21.014'**

The park is open for day use from Labor Day weekend through the last week in May and is closed during the summer months. Overnight camping is available year-round. Reservations are required, and there is a fee for parking. There are no defined trails starting at the campgrounds, but it's certainly possible for ghost hunters to undertake a short hike in any direction in search of shadowy spirits.

Contact the San Diego Department of Parks and Recreation for more information at sdparks.org/content/sdparks/en/park-pages/Vallecito .html. The website also has a link to the park brochure if you want to print it in advance.

46

The Cuyamaca Cryptid

Sweetwater River Loop Trail, Cuyamaca Rancho State Park
Descanso, San Diego County

CUYAMACA RANCHO STATE Park is located near the community of Descanso, about 40 miles east of San Diego and 25 miles north of the Mexican border. The property was acquired by the state in 1933. It contains just shy of 25,000 acres and has 137 miles of trails, including the trek to the summit of 5,730-foot Stonewall Peak. Hiking anywhere in the park is best between October and June.

Rangers warn visitors about the threat of mountain lions in the park, but the recreational area is also home to a reclusive cryptid that's been known to attack hikers. One of the places the curious creature is seen most often in Cuyamaca Rancho State Park is on Sweetwater River Loop Trail. Those who have run into the beast describe its body as being shaped like a human. It seems to be a biped, but then it will suddenly go down onto all fours. Plus, the animal is covered with snakelike scales, not fur or hair. The encounters are usually so terrifying that those who have escaped can't recall too many details. The monster may be nocturnal, because it only confronts backpackers after dark. So be careful not to wake the cryptid: A sign you may be close to its lair is seeing scattered bones or piles of crinkled, shed skin.

Haunted Trails

Sweetwater River Loop Trail is a 7.4-mile moderately trafficked path of moderate difficulty. The terrain changes constantly during the hike: rocks, boulders, waterfalls, meadows, and forest. There's a little something scenery-wise for everyone. **Trailhead GPS: N32 51.548' / W36 35.737'**

About 0.7 mile into your hike, the trail will split to form the loop. If you bear left when the branches separate, you'll shortly see a pleasant waterfall with several cascades. The falls are located about 1.5 miles from the trailhead. At this point, you'll also encounter the first of two river crossings on the loop. If you continue going clockwise, the second half of your hike will follow Sweetwater River as you head downhill toward the trailhead. The last 1.5 miles or so are also part of the Merigan Fire Road.

Some hikers prefer to do the loop counterclockwise. In this direction the first half of your trek will be uphill, but the grade isn't punishing. Your first river crossing will be about 3.1 miles into the trail, which will be followed by a hike up and over two back-to-back ridges. The last 2 miles of the trek will be almost completely downhill, capped by the second river crossing and seeing the waterfall.

No dogs are allowed on Sweetwater River Trail, but horseback riding is permitted. There's a fee to park in the lot on Viejas Boulevard near the trailhead. There may be free street parking nearby, but be sure to check signage before you leave your car unattended.

Although it seldom happens, during the wet season the river could be as high as your waist. By the end of the summer, the falls and river are sometimes completely dry.

47

The Forest Phantoms

Corte Madera Mountain Trail, Cleveland National Forest
Jumal, San Diego County

*Lawson Peak Trail, Lake Morena County Park Campground,
Cleveland National Forest*
Morena Village, San Diego County

CLEVELAND NATIONAL FOREST is big! Located about 30 miles east of San Diego, it occupies 460,000 acres, or 720 square miles, and it's the southernmost national forest in California. The park, named for President Grover Cleveland, was established in 1908 when Trabuco Canyon National Reserve and San Jacinto National Reserve were combined during the Theodore Roosevelt administration. An Adventure Pass is required to park in many places in the national forest.

At least two of the trails in Cleveland National Forest are said to be haunted. The first is Corte Madera Mountain Trail. The creatures appear around sunset, but no one is quite sure what they are. It's not even known whether they're human, animals, cryptids, or ghosts. From a distance they appear to be a bunch of boys aged from, say, 10 years old to their early teens. But as they come out of the brush and approach, hikers slowly realize that the enigmas have gigantic black eyes and faces covered with rodent-like whiskers. Given a chance they will attack, biting trekkers on the back and arms. If you see them, run!

The apparition that materializes on the second path, Lawson Peak Trail, is definitely a spirit, not flesh and bones. She's only been spotted after dark, and she has one very distinguishing feature: bloody sockets where her eyes should be. Her story is unknown. She's never hurt anyone on the trail, but running into her can be upsetting, to say the least.

If you're from out of the area and plan to hike Lawson Peak Trail from the south, you may want to consider staying overnight at the Lake Morena County Park Campground. (A section of the Pacific Coast Trail skirts the park as a possible bonus hike.) The campground has eighty-six sites, twenty of which are for tents only. Most of the RV and trailer sites have full or partial hookups. There are ten wilderness cabins available as well.

According to legend, the ghost of a young Woman in White strolls through the forested areas next to the campground. Even when visitors don't see the phantom, they sometimes hear her footsteps, laughter, or singing outside their tents at night. The spectre's identity remains unknown.

Some backpackers have reported that while camping elsewhere in Cleveland National Forest they found tiny, headless stick figures—effigies—sitting on the ground outside their tent flaps. If this happens to you, you might not want to take the little dolls home with you. Just in case.

Haunted Trails

Corte Madera Mountain Trail

Corte Madera Mountain Trail is probably best accessed from the small community of Jumal on CA 94. The trail is a heavily trafficked 6.4-mile out-and-back path, and it's rated as difficult. The route is partially paved, and dogs on a leash are allowed.

The hike actually starts on Espinosa Trail. **Trailhead GPS: N32 44.135' / W116 33.436'**

After about 1.5 miles, the path will hit a junction with Corte Madera Mountain Trail and Los Pinos Road. Veer right. After another 1,500 feet or so, the trail will split again. This time veer left to stay on Corte Madera Mountain Trail. From this point, you'll have about 1.5 more miles to the summit.

Lawson Peak Trail

Lawson Peak Trail is a 4.3-mile, lightly trafficked out-and-back hiking path rated as hard. There are options to reach the beginning of the trail. Most hikers start out from Morena Village, which is located on S 1. **Trailhead GPS: N32 42.810' / W116 42.344'**

The hike starts at a gate that blocks vehicular traffic. Walk around it. Until you reach the base of Lawson Peak, the trail is a washed-out service road. It's a steady climb all the way up, ending in a boulder scramble to the peak itself. There are usually ropes in place to assist your climb over some of the larger rocks. One of the hike's highlights is a cave near the summit.

Although cell phone service is generally good on the trail, hiking alone is highly discouraged. There's no signposting at the trailhead or any-where along the path. If the trail splits and there's a question as to which way to go, take the path that shows the most use. Dogs are allowed, but the going is tough for them on the final push.

48

The Omen

San Elijo Lagoon Nature Center Loop
Encinitas, San Diego County

Agua Hedionda Lagoon
Carlsbad, San Diego County

AN ELIJO LAGOON Ecological Reserve is a 979-acre estuary in Encinitas. It's located just south of the city's Cardiff beach community, where the Escondido and La Orilla Creeks meet the Pacific Ocean. The view changes constantly on the reserve's trails because much of the wetlands are covered by high tide twice a day.

The mutilated spectre of Maria, a little girl whose murdered body was discovered on the beach, wanders the trails and coastline of the San Elijo Lagoon Ecological Reserve. The youngster, who was polite and very religious, disappeared on her way to school. When her remains were later found on the shore, she was disfigured, which may be why her ghost is missing an eye, and her chin, jaw, and neck seem to be mashed together. Her killer was never found, but it's believed he or she was a homeless transient.

Spotting Maria's apparition is a bad omen: It means a relative or friend will soon become gravely ill and die. And don't make the mistake of approaching her if she calls for your help. She may have been sweet when she was alive, but now Maria's wraith seeks revenge for her death against everyone. If she catches hold of you, she'll drag you into the water and drown you.

Other than that, a stroll at Elijo Lagoon is delightful.

Agua Hedionda Lagoon is located on I-5 in Carlsbad just 10 miles north of San Elijo Lagoon. The recreation area, also known as Carlsbad Lagoon, is a saltwater wetland and is actually composed of three lakes, covering a total of 386 acres. Popular activities include boating, sailing, windsurfing, jet skiing, and fishing. There are nature trails and a few beaches as well. Allegedly, the firmest land in the park was used for a cemetery from 1885 to 1906. If so, that might explain the full-form apparitions and disembodied voices that are seen and heard around the lagoon.

Haunted Trails

The San Elijo Lagoon Nature Center Loop
There are 7 miles of easy-to-moderate trails within the San Elijo Lagoon Ecological Reserve suitable for all age and manner of hikers, and they can be hiked from sunrise to sunset. The San Elijo Lagoon Loop Trail can be accessed from several points around the preserve's nature center on Manchester Avenue. **Nature Center GPS: N33 00.804' / W117 16.456'**

The easy 0.5-mile trail is moderately trafficked, and part of it borders a river. This perimeter loop is more or less bisected by a path that cuts through the center of the marsh to give visitors a different perspective on the landscape.

The walk through the San Elijo Lagoon is a real treat for birders, and visitors will probably be able to see fish in the shallow waters as well. The outer pathway is lined with scrub, cacti, and chaparral, and there are benches here and there for those who want to sit for a while to take in the scenery. The loop's inner path passes through larger, denser vegetation. Dogs are permitted but must remain on a leash.

San Elijo Lagoon Nature Center
2710 Manchester Ave.
Cardiff, CA 92007
(760) 634-3026

49

Elfin Entities

Botanical Trail, Way Up Trail, Elfin Forest Recreational Reserve
Escondido, San Diego County

ELFIN FOREST IS an unincorporated residential community within the city of Escondido. The term "elfin forest" is one of several used by botanists to describe the type of short, mixed vegetation seen in the region. Mostly an elfin forest consists of bushes, scrub, and chaparral.

Elfin Forest Recreational Reserve was opened in 1992 to provide leisure opportunities for the public while also allowing San Diego County to manage its precious water and other natural resources.

The earliest inhabitants of the region were probably the Northern Diegueno. The San Diegueno and Luiseno later populated it as well. The Native Americans believed that the area had a positive, life-affirming aura. They called it their Peace Grounds, a neutral zone where members of different tribes could meet in harmony.

According to legend, the spirits of the North Diegueno still cling to their former land. On occasion, their ghosts are seen hanging from the trees. The revenant of a one-armed, nonnative man sometimes stands close to the trailhead as if he's ready to chase off vandals or anyone else who would spoil the property. You may also spot a 10-foot-long phantom white owl flying overhead between the hours of midnight and 2 a.m.

The spectre of a woman dubbed the White Lady roams through the reserve trying to find her husband and child, who were supposedly killed there by an assailant. Ghost investigators suggest she may be looking for the murderer instead. Both hikers and those driving on Harmony Grove Road have spotted the woman's apparition floating about a foot off the ground. Also called the White Witch, she's been known to touch hikers, sometimes gripping them at the back of their skulls hard enough to draw blood.

Finally, there are claims of stone circles scattered throughout the park. If they exist—so far there's no photographic evidence—they could possibly be the sites of ancient tribal rituals. Or maybe they're Indian burial grounds. For some reason, a few paranormal theorists have speculated that the circles are actually "time tunnels" to and from the past.

Haunted Trails

Botanical Trail is a great introductory hike to the Elfin Forest Recreational Reserve. It's an easy 1.1-mile loop that's heavily trafficked. The trailhead is on one side of the parking lot on Harmony Grove Road. The lot is free but small. You may have to look for street parking. As always, check restrictions on signage if you do the latter. Be sure to check out the visitor center in the parking area before or after your hike. Leashed dogs are okay on the trail. **Botanical Trailhead GPS: N33 05.196' / W117 08.717'**

Shortly after setting out on the trail, you'll cross Escondido Creek. (Don't try to ford the stream if it's been swollen by rain or winter melt-off.) The shaded path has twenty-seven markers along the route identifying the foliage that correspond to a nature guide that's available on-site or online at olivenhain.com/files/docs/Park/BotanicMap/MapBotanical/story.html.

Way Up Trail shares a trailhead with Botanical Trail, but it branches off about halfway around the latter's loop. It climbs about 0.9 mile to reach Harmony Grove Overlook, where there's an expansive view of Olivenhain Reservoir. Way Up Trail is moderately trafficked, and it has been rated easy, but the section between Botanical Trail and the overlook is steep with lots of switchbacks. **Way Up Trail / Botanical Trail Split GPS: N33 05.129' / W117 08.508'**

The 784-acre Elfin Forest Recreational Reserve has approximately 11 miles of trails for hiking, mountain biking, and equestrian use. It's open daily except December 25 from 8 a.m. to about a half hour before sunset. (Hours are signposted each day.) The park is closed on rainy days and when there are red-flag warnings due to a high possibility of fire.

50

The Snake Maiden

Beach Trail, Broken Hill Trail, Guy Fleming Trail, Razor Point Trail, Torrey Pines State Natural Reserve, Windansea Beach
La Jolla, San Diego County

NE OF THE most unspoiled pieces of property in Southern California is the Torrey Pines State Natural Reserve. More than 2,000 coastal acres just north of La Jolla, the park was designated a National Natural Landmark in 1977. It began in 1899 as the vision of one man, retailer and philanthropist George Marston, who convinced the San Diego City Council to set aside 364 acres north of downtown. Through donations of land and money, the reserve has grown steadily over the years to its present size of more than 3 square miles. Originally the park was under local management, but in 1956 ownership of the land was turned over to the state, which was better equipped to administer it.

The place is windswept and rugged. There's the long, pristine beach, of course, and a large lagoon and marsh protected by a horseshoe-shaped plateau whose opening faces the sea. The area looks almost exactly the way it did when it was a hunting ground and habitat of the native Kumeyaay people. Now it's home to seabirds, a wide variety of land mammals from rabbits to bobcats, and flora such as sage, chaparral, and cacti. Its most important treasure is the unique and endangered Torrey pine, the rarest type of pine tree in North America. This particular subspecies grows nowhere else in the world.

The ghost of a Native American girl roams the Torrey Pines trails, looking for victims. Her name is Chu-mana, which roughly translates from the Hopi as "Snake Maiden." The name is apt because she has a forked tongue. Also she has no eyes. She appears at sundown, only when there's a quarter moon, looking to steal the eyes of some unfortunate, unsuspecting hiker. Be especially wary if you take the hike out to Broken Hill. The isolated peak is her favorite spot to haunt.

If you drop south to La Jolla itself, you'll come to Windansea Beach. Located between Westbourne Street (to the north) and Palomar Avenue, the stretch of sand as well as the neighborhood is named for an ocean-front hotel that once stood there. From 1909 to 1919 it was known as the Strand Hotel; from then until its closure in 1943 it was called the Windansea Hotel.

Windansea Beach is a reef break, which means its waves break over an underground reef as they come in. In the winter months, breaks at the beach are usually a modest 6 to 8 feet in height—no record, but still very surfable.

Which brings us to the ghosts. The apparitions of two different men have been seen (or sometimes only sensed) surfing the waves at Windansea Beach. One of the spectres is believed to be Bob Simmons, who became renowned for redesigning and shaping surfboards. He drowned while surfing at Windansea in 1954 at the age of 35. The other phantom is Chris O'Rourke, a brilliant competitive surfer, who died of Hodgkin's lymphoma in 1981 when he was only 22 years old. His ashes were scattered in the ocean just off Windansea Beach. According to those who have seen or felt their presence, both spirits exude good vibes whenever they're around.

Haunted Trails

There are 8 miles of established trails in Torrey Pines State Natural Reserve. Beach Trail is an easy 0.75-mile path down to the water. It's not overly scenic, but when you get to the end of it, hey, you're at the ocean! **Trailhead GPS: N32 55.582' / W117 15.546'**

(Perhaps of interest, at the southern end of Torrey Pines State Beach there's a boulder known as Flat Rock jutting out into the Pacific. On the other side of that giant stone is Black's Beach, San Diego's unofficial nude beach.)

If you want, you can extend your Beach Trail hike into a 2.3-mile heavily trafficked loop by walking the beach south to Yucca Point, then hiking up the cliff and back to the trailhead via Red Butte and High Point.

Broken Hill Trail is 2.3-mile loop trail that takes in both the Broken Hill Overlook and nearby Yucca Point. The hike is moderate, but it is heavily trafficked year-round. The trailhead is off Torrey Pines Road. **Trailhead GPS: N32 54.862' / W117 15.684'**

Guy Fleming Trail is an easy, moderately trafficked 0.8-mile loop. There are plentiful wildflowers in season, and many people hike the path in the winter for whale watching. **Trailhead GPS: N32 55.393' / W117 15.298'**

Razor Point Trail is another easy trail for visitors to Torrey Pines State Natural Reserve. It's a 1.3-mile out-and-back trail featuring sage scrub and sandstone gorges. **Trailhead GPS: N32 55.197' / W117 15.179'**

Be cautious at all times. All of the cliffs in Torrey Pines State Natural Reserve are unstable, whether dry or wet, and even bluffs that seem solidly packed can collapse without warning. Also, no dogs are allowed on any of these trails.

51

The Invisible Interlopers

Pyles Peak, Mission Trails Regional Park
San Diego, San Diego County

MISSION TRAILS REGIONAL Park is a large open-space preserve that lies on land once inhabited by Kumeyaay. It's located in Greater San Diego to the northeast of downtown. The recreational area was opened in 1974, and with 7,720 acres, it's one of the largest city-owned parks in the country. There are about 60 miles of trails for hikers, mountain bikers, and equestrians. Leashed dogs are also allowed. The land is covered with brush and chaparral, and there is no shade.

The park has five major mountain peaks: Cowles Mountain, Pyles Peak, Kwaay Paay Peak, South Fortuna, and North Fortuna. Park rangers Levi Dean and Heidi Gutknecht have created a 5-Peak Challenge to encourage hikers to conquer all five summits. (For more information on the program, trail maps, or other park details, visit the park's website at mtrp.org.)

The park's highest point—and the highest in the city—is Cowles Mountain, which stands at 1,592 feet. The peak is named for George A. Cowles, a San Diego County rancher and businessman in the 1870s and 1880s.

Kenneth Pyle, chief cartographer for the San Diego County Planning Department in the 1970s, named Pyles Peak for himself. After hiking to the crest of Cowles Mountain, it's possible to continue on the trail until you reach Pyles Peak, yet surprisingly few people do—despite the fact that the hike is of moderate difficulty, and the path is often surrounded by fields of wildflowers. Could it be that hikers are reluctant to tackle another steep hillside right away? Or could it be because of the ghosts?

As you approach the top of Pyles Peak, invisible spirits come out to play, even in the daytime. Hikers occasionally feel invisible hands tug at their belongings or fingers wrap around their throats. Inexplicable bite marks appear on their legs, sometimes even on their inner thighs! Also, many dogs have stopped in their tracks after passing Cowles Mountain and refuse to go any farther. They've even been known to force their owners to turn back. (It's long been believed that animals are particularly sensitive to unseen entities, and Pyles Peak Trail doesn't disappoint.)

So far there's been no hint as to the identity of the phantoms or why they're being such a nuisance. Perhaps in this case, ignorance is bliss.

Haunted Trails

The hike to the top of Cowles Mountain is 2.9 miles out and back, and it's of moderate difficulty. It's the park's most popular hike by far because of the 360-degree view from the summit. On very clear days, it's possible to see Mexico to the south and all the way north to Orange County! The Cowles Mountain trailhead is in the San Carlos neighborhood of San Diego at the intersection of Golfcrest Drive and Navajo Road. **Trailhead GPS: N32 48.292' / W117 02.250'**

Pyles Peak shares its trailhead with Cowles Mountain. The hike all the way to Pyles Peak is 5.3 miles out and back.

Bibliography

A full list of the books consulted during the preparation of *Spooky Trails* is too extensive to include, so I'm nominating just three works that I consider essential to any hiker who is also a would-be ghost hunter. The first, by Dennis Hauck, has become a classic, and it describes hauntings in all sorts of venues across the United States. The other two books focus on hiking trails or backpacking destinations.

Books

Hauck, Dennis William. *Haunted Places: The National Directory*. New York: Penguin, 1996. *The National Directory* is one of the most popular "ghost books" in print. It's an easy-to-use reference book that lists its haunted sites by state and city in A-to-Z order.

Horjust, Maren. *Haunted Hikes: Real Life Stories of Paranormal Activity in the Woods*. Guilford, CT: FalconGuides, 2017. This 228-page book has one hundred short chapters, each one detailing a specific hiking trail. The work is separated into eight regions of the United States. Each chapter ends with the location of or directions to the trailhead as well as a few pertinent facts regarding the hike. Most of the tales take place in state parks or wilderness areas.

Lankford, Andrea. *Haunted Hikes: Spine-Tingling Tales and Trails from North America's National Parks*. Santa Monica, CA: Santa Monica Press, 2006. This 373-page paperback contains fifty-one short chapters sorted into eight regional sections of the United States and Canada. The length of the ghost stories varies. There are numerous black-and-white photographs, full- and half-page maps of recommended hikes, and descriptions of the trails.

Video

No commercial video seems to explore haunted hiking trails as its primary subject. Backpackers, members of paranormal societies, and solo ghost hunters, however, have posted countless personal videos of their adventures on social media, especially on YouTube. These self-produced videos visually document their hikes as they go in search of the Unknown.

Some of the videos concentrate on the history of the ghost legend rather than the hike itself, such as the video I produced about the haunted HOLLYWOOD sign found at https://www.youtube.com/watch?v=ROSPOJrV0eM&t=3s.

The key words to search online for such videos are the name of a trail or its general location and the word "ghost," "haunted," or some similar term. You'll find plenty of choices, some of them pretty scary. You may not want to watch them alone in the dark.

Websites

In addition to books and video, I consulted more than a hundred websites during my research for this book. The sites fell into four main categories, so here are a couple of examples of each type.

Administrators

Site managed by the agency that maintains the trail.

nps.gov/yose/planyourvisit/bridalveilfalltrail.htm
Bridalveil Fall Trail
Yosemite National Park

BIBLIOGRAPHY

boyscouts-marin.org
Tamarancho Trail
Marin Council of the Boy Scouts of America
Fairfax

Hiking Organizations
Sites managed by outdoor enthusiasts.

AllTrails.com
If you're a devoted hiker, backpacker, or camper, you're probably already familiar with AllTrails.com. The site offers general and technical information about established trails, including the pathway's condition, restrictions, maps, and trailhead GPS, as well as reviews and recommendations from past visitors.

backpackerverse.com
This site is designed for hikers who are also ghost aficionados. You'll find spooky stories, hiking tips, and several Top Ten–style lists of haunted trails.

Directories
There are several paranormal websites that collect ghost stories from users, create thumbnail sketches of the haunted places, and list them alphabetically by county, state, and city. This type of aggregator site constantly changes as users update the existing tales or add new ones. Some directory sites contain thousands of listings.

theshadowlands.net
Online since 1994. Founded by Dave Juliano.

haunted-places.com

Paranormal Investigators

Many ghost hunters and research societies, authors, and speakers on spirit phenomena have websites where they recount their otherworldly experiences or offer their services. Some of them limit their sites or services to a particular city or region.

hauntedoc.com
Ernie Alonzo
Haunted Orange County
Working with historian Charles Spratley, Ernie Alonzo founded Haunted Orange County. The organization operates ghost walks, talks, and paranormal-related special events in the O.C. Among their offerings is a 2.5-hour Black Star Canyon Ghost Walk.

ghoula.blogspot.com
Richard Carradine
GHOULA
Historian-researcher-author Richard Carradine founded Ghost Hunters of Urban Los Angeles (GHOULA) in 2006 to give fellow ghost enthusiasts a way to share their experiences. For many years, he also hosted "Spirits with Spirits," a casual meet-up on the 13th of each month at a different haunted bar or restaurant somewhere in Greater Los Angeles.

richardsenate.com
Richard Senate
Richard Senate, one the best-known ghost hunters in Southern California, has spent a lifetime investigating hauntings, writing, lecturing, and giving ghost tours in the Golden State.

theghostguy.com
Tom Ogden
The author's website, covering all things paranormal.

About the Author

Tom Ogden is one of America's leading experts on the paranormal, and, as a professional magician for the past forty years, he has a special insight into ghost phenomena, hauntings, and things that go bump in the night.

Ogden's first book, *200 Years of the American Circus*, was released in 1994. The American Library Association and the New York Public Library named it a "Best Reference Work," and Tom was subsequently profiled in *Writer's Market*. Ogden's other early books include *Wizards and Sorcerers* and two instructional magic books for the *Complete Idiot's Guide* series.

In 1998 Tom Ogden released *The Complete Idiot's Guide to Ghosts and Hauntings*, now in its second edition. A recent expanded volume of *Haunted Cemeteries* was his eleventh book of ghost stories for Globe Pequot's "Haunted" series. *Spooky Trails and Tall Tales California* is Tom's first work for FalconGuides.

Nicknamed "The Ghost Guy," Ogden has been interviewed on numerous radio programs and podcasts, and he's in demand as a speaker on the Spirit World. His original ghost videos can be found on YouTube, and he's a member of the Paranormal Investigation Committee of the Society of American Magicians.

Tom Ogden resides in haunted Hollywood, California.

CPSIA information can be obtained
at www.ICGtesting.com
Printed in the USA
LVHW040446081222
734767LV00002B/350